UNDERSTANDING THE PURPOSE AND POWER OF

PRAYER

Study Guide

DR. MYLES MUNROE

WHITAKER
HOUSE

UNDERSTANDING THE PURPOSE AND POWER OF PRAYER
STUDY GUIDE

Dr. Myles Munroe
Bahamas Faith Ministries International
P.O. Box N9583
Nassau, Bahamas
e-mail: bfmadmin@bfmmm.com
website: www.bfmmm.com

ISBN: 0-88368-856-5
Printed in the United States of America
© 2003 by Dr. Myles Munroe

Whitaker House
30 Hunt Valley Circle
New Kensington, PA 15068
website: www.whitakerhouse.com

Library of Congress Cataloging-in-Publication Data
Munroe, Myles.
Understanding the purpose and power of prayer. Study guide/
Myles Munroe.
p. cm.
ISBN 0-88368-856-5 (pbk.)
1. Prayer. I. Title.
BV215.M833 2003
248.3'2—dc22
2003014591

2 3 4 5 6 7 8 9 10 11 12 **U** 11 10 09 08 07 06 05 04

UNDERSTANDING THE PURPOSE AND POWER OF

PRAYER

Study Guide

Other books by Dr. Myles Munroe

The Principles and Power of Vision
The Principles and Power of Vision Study Guide
Understanding the Purpose and Power of Men
Understanding the Purpose and Power of Men Study Guide
Understanding the Purpose and Power of Prayer
Understanding the Purpose and Power of Prayer Study Guide
Understanding the Purpose and Power of Woman
Understanding the Purpose and Power of Woman Study Guide

Available in Spanish

Entendiendo el propósito y el poder de la mujer
(Understanding the Purpose and Power of Woman)

Entendiendo el propósito y el poder de los hombres
(Understanding the Purpose and Power of Men)

Los principios y el poder de la visión
(The Principles and Power of Vision)

Contents

How to Use This
Study Guide

This study guide complement to *Understanding the Purpose and Power of Prayer* by Dr. Myles Munroe may be used for individual reflection and spiritual growth or Bible study and Sunday school discussion. The study can be easily adapted to suit your particular needs or the needs of a group. For your convenience, an answer key is provided in the back of this study guide.

Each chapter review in this guide includes the following elements:

Chapter Theme: The main idea of each chapter is summarized for emphasis and clarity.

Questions for Reflection: One or more questions are given as a warm-up to lead into the study or discussion of the topic. (For group study, these questions may be asked before or after reading the Chapter Theme, at the leader's discretion.)

Exploring God's Principles and Purposes: Questions and review material are provided that highlight and summarize the truths and principles within each chapter and begin to lead the reader/group participant to personalize what is being studied. Page numbers corresponding to the book are listed for easy reference.

Conclusion: A summary or implication statement is included to put the chapter theme into perspective.

Applying God's Principles to Your Life: Thought-provoking questions and suggestions for prayer and personal action are provided to help the individual/group participant apply the study material to his or her particular life circumstances. This section includes three parts:

- Thinking It Over
- Praying about It
- Acting on God's Truth

As you progress through *Understanding the Purpose and Power of Prayer* and review the truths and principles through this study guide, you will find that you can make a difference in this world and even change the course of history by following God's guidelines for prayer. Join Dr. Munroe on an adventure into the heart of prayer and experience a dynamic life of purposeful petition for heavenly impact on earth.

Introduction

Ican remember many times in the past when I attended prayer meetings and, while I was praying, wondered whether it was worth it or if prayer really worked at all. Even as a Christian leader, sometimes I went through only the motions of prayer, with no real belief in what I was participating in.

I am certain that my struggles with the prayer issue were not unique to me. I have spoken with countless individuals who have also grappled with it. Some still strive to understand its practice and to believe in its validity.

Many are suffering from a silent disillusionment with their experience of prayer. They have secretly asked themselves these questions: "Does prayer really work? Is someone listening? Does it make a difference? Can it truly change circumstances?" They are afraid to ask these questions openly for fear that others will think they are "unspiritual" or because they feel something is wrong with them. Therefore, they practice prayer but don't fully believe in it; for them, prayer has become only a ritual with no reality. Many more have simply abandoned the practice.

Perhaps many of us avoid prayer because the human spirit hates failure and disappointment. To many people, prayer is like putting money into a soda machine that doesn't give a can of soda in return: You stand in front of it and become increasingly frustrated until you finally kick it and walk away. The significant thing is that you will probably never attempt to use it again. Many people feel they have put in too many prayer coins and received too few satisfying answers.

Despite all the questions, confusion, and uncertainty surrounding prayer, it is still one of the greatest common denominators among all the great Bible characters and thousands of believers throughout history. Moses and Abraham practiced it. David, Solomon, Esther, Deborah, Daniel, Joseph, all the prophets—and, of course, Jesus Christ Himself—had dynamic and profound commitments to prayer. Their records, and the records of numbers of Christians through the ages, show the direct impact of prayer on their lives and on the circumstances they faced. The evidence affirms that one thing is sure: No matter what you may think about prayer, somehow it has worked for others. Why not everyone?

The question is not whether prayer is valid or effective, but this: Do we understand it and know how it works? It was not until I learned the principles of purpose and faithfulness that I began to grasp the nature, philosophy, and foundation of prayer and to experience the power and positive results of prayer in my own life. We must understand the source, principles, and purpose of prayer to learn the answers to these questions: What is prayer? Why is it necessary? How should we pray? Why do we pray to God in the name of Jesus? Why is prayer not always answered in the way we expect? When should we stop praying? What role does faith have in the prayer process? Do we have to "qualify" to pray? Does prayer affect or change destiny? If God is sovereign and can do whatever He wishes, then why pray in the first place?

When we study the Bible, we see that every action taken by God in the earthly realm required the involvement of a human being and his or her prayers. To rescue humanity in the Flood, He needed Noah. For the creation of a nation, He needed Abraham. To lead the nation of Israel, He needed Moses. To defeat Jericho, He needed Joshua. To help bring back Israel from captivity, He needed Daniel. For the preservation of the Hebrews, He needed Esther. For the salvation of mankind, *He needed to become a man.*

Prayer is therefore not an option for humanity but a necessity. If we don't pray, heaven will not "interfere" in earth's affairs. It is imperative that we take responsibility and determine what happens on the earth by our prayer lives.

This is the challenge that we will embrace as we explore the principles and precepts established by the Creator regarding prayer and discover the keys to unlocking its purpose and power. Let us begin by taking a journey through the land of doubt, shedding the skepticism and activating the most awesome power every human being possesses: the power to influence earth from heaven through prayer.

—Myles Munroe

Part I
The Purpose and Priority of Prayer

Chapter One

Does Prayer Really Work?

Prayer is one of the most misunderstood arts of the human experience—yet it is meant to be one of the most exciting aspects of a life of faith.

CHAPTER THEME

The power of prayer is the inheritance of the believer, and it is meant to be one of the most exciting aspects of a life of faith. Prayer transforms lives, changes circumstances, gives peace and perseverance in the midst of trial, alters the course of nations, and wins the world for Christ. Yet prayer is one of the most misunderstood arts of the human experience. Confusion over how prayer "works" has led to discouragement and disillusionment in believers, undermining their relationships with God and causing them to be ineffective in His service. Yet when believers recognize the obstacles that prevent prayer from being answered and learn the biblical principles of prayer, they can have a close relationship with their heavenly Father as they serve Him with joy and effectiveness.

Questions for Reflection

1. What is your practice of prayer? (For example: How often do you pray? Do you use a certain method when you pray? Do you pray at certain times of the day?)

2. Do you feel that you receive answers to your prayers? Why or why not?

3. If you haven't felt that your prayers have been answered (either in general or in a specific situation), what effect has this had on you? How has it made you feel about prayer, God, and yourself?

4. What aspects of prayer are confusing or unclear to you?

Exploring God's Principles and Purposes

5. What is a major obstacle that stands in the way of a life of true faith? (p. 19)

   unanswered   prayer

6. For many people, the practice of prayer is merely a religious   exercise   , one that isn't concerned with obtaining results . (p. 20)

7. What is one way we can measure how much the average Christian believes in the effectiveness of prayer? (p. 20)

   By how many people attend prayer meetings

8. In general, there is a lack of _teaching_, _interest_, and _understanding_ about prayer in the church. (p. 20)

9. What are some reasons that a great many believers don't have successful prayer lives? (p. 22)

10. List five consequences of unanswered prayer: (pp. 21–22)

    1. _The feeling of abandonment and isolation from God_

    2. _Questioning God's character and integrity_

    3. _Feeling that our lives are unsettled and unstable_

    4. _Premature conclusions about ourselves and our prayers_

    5. _Doubting our calling as God's intercessors_

11. What are some effects of confusion over prayer? (p. 22)
    Powerlessness, Lack of Direction, Little victory over sin, poverty, Poor Spiritual progress

12. True prayer is— [choose one] (p. 22)

    (a) an activity.
    (b) a ritual or obligation.
    (c) communion and communication with God that touches His heart.
    (d) begging God to do what we want Him to do.

13. What does prayer have the power to do? (p. 22)
    Transform Lives, Change Circumstances, give peace + Perseverance in the midst of trials, alter the course of nations + win the world for Christ

14. The power of prayer is the _inheritance_ of the believer. (p. 23)

15. Circle one: (True) or False

    When prayer does not bring results, it is an indication that something is wrong. (p. 23)

16. Circle one: True or (False)

    The answers to our prayers will always be immediately manifested. (p. 23)

17. What assurance did Jesus give us that God does hear and answer prayer? (p. 24) *He said so !*
    Mark 11:24   *& He is Faithful*

18. Under what circumstances do God's will and Word work in our lives? (p. 24)
    When they are understood + put into practice

19. What results does true prayer bring about? (p. 24)
    - Building Intimacy w/ God   *- Cause a trust in His Love*
    - Honor to Him   *- Affirm His purposes + will*
    - Respect for His integrity
    - Enable belief in His Word   *- Appropriate His promises*

20. Why does God sometimes withhold answers to our prayers? (pp. 24–25) *So we will seek Him*

21. Praying without understanding or applying the principles of prayer is usually *ineffective* . (p. 25)

22. Complete the following: "Prayer is meant to be answered— *or else God would not ask us to pray* ." (p. 25)

23. How do we know that Jesus always expected His prayers to be heard by God the Father? (p. 25)
    He (God) said so! John 11:41+42
    Prayer is meant to be answered or He wouldnt

Conclusion
    ask us to pray!

Believers are called to be God's priests and ambassadors in the world through prayer and intercession. You can have an effective prayer life that will overflow into all other areas of your life when you discover how to approach God and learn the kind of prayers God responds to. It is God's desire that you experience intimacy with Him and spiritual strength to fulfill His purposes. When you understand the biblical principles of the art of prayer, you will begin to communicate with God with power, grace, and confidence. These principles will help you to clear away the obstacle of unanswered prayer so that you can enter into a new dimension of faith, deep love for God, and power for service.

Applying God's Principles to Your Life

Thinking It Over

- Which of the following *best* describes the current role of prayer in your life?

    —a religious exercise or ritual

    —an obligation that feels burdensome

    —meaningful communion and intercession with God

    —a nonexistent role

- How has your perspective of prayer/unanswered prayer changed as a result of reading this chapter?

- Are you experiencing any of the following in your life: powerlessness, lack of direction, little victory over sin, poor spiritual progress, a weak witness, unfruitful ministry, poverty, or other similar problems? If so, how would a greater knowledge and understanding about prayer make a difference in your life?

Praying about It

- Have disappointments and confusion over unanswered prayer caused you to abandon or lessen your practice of prayer? Be honest with God about how unanswered prayer has made you feel about prayer, yourself, and Him. Ask God to forgive you if you have been bitter toward Him because of unanswered prayer, to restore you to a right relationship with Him, and to help you better understand His purposes and principles for answered prayer.

- In Luke 18:1, Jesus said that we *"should always pray and not give up."* If you have abandoned the practice of prayer, begin to renew your fellowship with God by praying for a short time every morning and as needs arise throughout the day. Trust God to reveal His answers to you in His timing, with the knowledge that He loves and cares for you. *"Casting all your care upon Him, for He cares for you"* (1 Peter 5:7 NKJV).

Acting on God's Truth

- What is your primary question about the role of prayer in the life of the Christian? Write down your question on a piece of paper and then, below it, write down what you learn throughout this study that addresses this question.

- As you go through this study, begin to incorporate the principles you learn about prayer into your daily prayer life, one at a time.

God does nothing but in answer to prayer.
—John Wesley*

* Quoted in E. M. Bounds, *Power through Prayer*, Chapter 11, "The Example of the Apostles," published by Whitaker House.

Chapter Two

The Genesis of Prayer

Prayer is mankind exercising dominion on the earth by giving
God the freedom to intervene in earth's affairs.

CHAPTER THEME

We need to understand essential truths about God's nature and His purposes for mankind that lead to the necessity of prayer. The biblical account of the creation of humanity reveals these truths.

Question for Reflection

1. If God is all-knowing and all-powerful, why do we need to pray?

Exploring God's Principles and Purposes

2. Complete the following: God is a God of <u>purpose</u>.
   His actions are not <u>arbitrary</u>. (p. 29)

3. In Genesis 1:26, God said, *"Let us make man in our image, in our likeness, and let them rule."* What two truths does this statement reveal about God's purposes for humanity in relation to prayer? (pp. 30–32) ① Because God created us to reflect His character + personality, He designed us to find fulfillment + ultimate meaning in <u>Him</u>. We were intended

   ② We were created to share in God's authority over the earth. Man was meant to carry out God's purposes for the earth using our own will + initiative.

4. In what manner does God want us to approach Him? (p. 30) God wants us to approach Him as a child would a loving Father

5. God gave humanity free will. What are the implications of this gift in regard to dominion? (p. 31)
   Man was given the ability to plan and make decisions, and then to take action to fulfill those plans, just as God did in creating the world

6. In what two realms is humanity to carry out dominion over the earth? (pp. 32–34)
   The Earthly Realm + The Spiritual Realm

7. What is the overarching meaning of this dual dominion? What verse emphasizes this truth? (p. 34) God wanted/(wants) us to take the character of the Garden of Eden – God's Presence, light, + truth – and spread it throughout the world. "The earth will be full of the knowledge of the Lord as the waters cover the sea." Isaiah 11:9

8. We can function in the purposes for which we were created only as we are <u>connected</u> to God, our Source. (p. 33)

9. God doesn't want mankind to work <u>for</u> Him, but rather <u>with</u> Him. (p. 34)

10. When God created mankind to share His authority, it was in the context of humanity's relationship to Him as His offspring_____. God didn't create men and women to be servents_____, but to be sons_____ and daughters_____ who share His purposes and desire to fulfill them. (p. 34)

11. What does the meaning of the original Greek signify about our being *"God's fellow workers"* (2 Cor. 6:1)? (p. 34)
"Fellow Workers" means those who "cooperate", who "help with", who "work together"

12. What do some people say is the reason prayer originated? (p. 35)

13. Why is this reason *not* the essence of true prayer? (p. 35)

14. To review, in light of mankind's purpose, what is the twofold essence of prayer? (p. 35)

15. What does it mean to have union with God? (p. 35)

16. Prayer is the medium through which the human spirit _____ and is _____ _____ the will and purpose of the divine Creator. (p. 36)

17. What did Dr. Munroe say formed the essence of the very first prayer? (p. 36)

18. Why did Adam pray when he was already in the presence of God? (p. 36)

19. Why is prayer essential for God's will to be done in the earth? (p. 37)

20. Prayer is _____ (not _____) for spiritual progress and victory in our individual lives and in the world at large. (p. 37)

21. In light of the earthly authority God has given mankind, what is another important definition of prayer? (p. 38)

22. God's will is meant to be the _____ and _____ of your prayers, the _____ of your intercession, the _____ of your confidence in supplication, the _____ of your fervent and effectual prayers. (p. 38)

23. Complete the following: Praying does not mean convincing God to do your will, but doing _____ _____. (p. 38)

24. What is the key to effective prayer? (p. 38)

25. Once you understand your purpose, what does it become in regard to your prayers? (p. 38)

26. Prayer is calling forth what God has already _____ and _____—continuing His work of creation and the establishment of His plans for the earth. (p. 38)

27. Why do we often pray in the wrong way? (p. 39)

28. What was Jesus' assurance in prayer based on? (p. 40)

29. When we know God's will, when we are obedient to it, and when we ask God to fulfill it, what happens? (p. 40)

30. What happens when we stop praying? (pp. 40–41)

31. Circle one: True or False

    God will ultimately bring His purposes to pass in the world—with or without our cooperation. (p. 41)

32. When we neglect to pray, what are we failing to fulfill? (p. 41)

33. What happens when man (humanity) uses his will for anything other than God's will? (p. 41)

34. If God gave mankind dominion over the earth, why does the Bible refer to Satan as *"the god of this world"* (2 Cor. 4:4 KJV)? (pp. 41–42)

35. When Adam and Eve broke their relationship with God, how was their effectiveness in prayer affected? (p. 42)

36. When we pray, we represent God's interests on earth, and representation requires _____. (p. 42)

37. To what can our difficulties in prayer be traced? (p. 42)

38. Why is prayer an area in which we need to be *"transformed by the renewing of* [our] *mind"* (Rom. 12:2 KJV)? (p. 42)

Conclusion

Prayer is not an option for the believer. It is a necessity for our relationship with God and for fulfilling His purposes in the world and in our individual lives. Time spent in prayer is not time wasted but time invested. As we embrace the will of God, as we live before Him in the righteousness of Christ, and as we seek to fulfill His purposes, nothing will be able to hinder our prayers, and we will begin to understand Jesus' saying, *"With God all things are possible"* (Matt. 19:26).

Applying God's Principles to Your Life

Thinking It Over

• Have you ever neglected to pray because you felt God would do whatever He wanted to do anyway? If so, how has your perspective about this changed after reading this chapter?

• When we pray, we represent God's interests on earth, and representation requires relationship. What can you do today to build a deeper relationship of love with God?

• In what ways do you need to renew your mind in regard to prayer?

Praying about It

- With what attitude or perspective do you usually go to God in prayer? God wants us to approach Him as a child would a loving father. This week, pray to God recognizing Him as your loving heavenly Father. If this approach is new to you, it may seem awkward at first, but make it a practice in your prayers. Over time, note the difference that this new approach to God makes in your relationship with Him and in the content of your prayers.

- Praying does not mean convincing God to do your will, but doing His will through your will. Are there any areas in your life in which you have been resisting God's will? If so, surrender these areas to God and ask Him to fulfill His purposes in your life so you can help fulfill His purposes in the world.

- If you have never trusted in Christ to restore your broken relationship with God, pray to the Father now, acknowledging your belief in Christ as your Savior from sin, and your trust in God's love and forgiveness on the basis of Christ's death for you on the cross. Ask God to fill you with His Holy Spirit and to enable you to live a life that pleases Him and fulfills His purposes. Then, thank God for making you *"a new creation"* (2 Cor. 5:17) as you seek to live for Him daily.

Acting on God's Truth

- Prayer should not be open-ended but purpose-driven, motivated by a knowledge of God's ways and intentions. Therefore, the key to effective prayer is understanding God's purpose for the world and for your life—His reason for your existence as a human being in general and as an individual specifically. How well do you know God's purposes for yourself and the world? What will you do to learn more about these purposes?

- If we don't ask God to intervene in human affairs, our world will be susceptible to the influences of Satan and sin. God's plan is for mankind to desire what He desires, to will what He wills, and to ask Him to accomplish His purposes so that goodness and truth may reign on the earth rather than evil and darkness. This week, focus on one of God's purposes and begin to agree with Him about it in prayer.

• Commit the following verses to memory:

This is the confidence we have in approaching God: that if we ask anything according to his will, he hears us. And if we know that he hears us—whatever we ask—we know that we have what we asked of him.
(1 John 5:14–15)

Not my will, but yours be done. (Luke 22:42)

The heart of prayer is communion with God in a unity of love and purpose.

Chapter Three
The Authority of Prayer

The position and authority that Jesus won have been transferred back to mankind through spiritual rebirth in Christ.

CHAPTER THEME

God originally gave humanity the right to pray by virtue of man's relationship with Him and his purpose of exercising dominion over the earth. Yet our relationship with our Creator was broken, and our dominion authority was forfeited, by our first ancestors. The result was that Satan, rather than man, became *"the god of this world"* (2 Cor. 4:4 KJV). What now gives us the right to pray? Becoming sure of the answer to that question in your own heart and mind is essential if you are to have an effective prayer life.

Questions for Reflection

1. Why do you pray?

2. On what basis do you have a right to pray?

Exploring God's Principles and Purposes

3. Through the fall of mankind, people became estranged from God and His plans for humanity so that they— [choose one] (p. 47)

   (a) felt isolated from God.

   (b) were unsure of where they stood with God.

   (c) didn't know what God wanted to do for and through them.

   (d) lost their sense of purpose.

   (e) all of the above

4. If the above descriptions in "a" through "d" remind you of your own prayer life, what can you conclude about the way you view prayer? (p. 48)

5. When mankind rebelled against God and turned the world's authority over to Satan, why didn't God simply come down and wrench control of the earth back from the devil? (p. 48)

6. What needed to be accomplished in order to ensure man's restoration? (p. 48)

7. Complete the following: Only through Christ are we restored to our _____ in God, and only through Christ do we have a right to _____ with _____. (p. 49)

8. According to Ephesians 3:12, how may we approach God when we do so through faith in Christ? (p. 49)

9. What is the only way in which Jesus could restore God's purpose to mankind? (p. 49)

10. What is the only way in which Jesus could reestablish mankind's relationship with God? (pp. 49–50)

11. There are six qualities Christ manifested as the Second Adam. What is the first one? (p. 50)

12. The fullness of the *"image of God"* (2 Cor. 4:4) was revealed in both Christ's _____ and His _____. (p. 50)

13. What is the second quality Christ manifested as the Second Adam? (p. 50)

14. The love of the Father and the Son is so deep and reciprocal that Jesus could say, "_____ _____" (John 10:30). (p. 51)

15. The third quality Christ manifested as the Second Adam is that _____. (p. 51)

16. What does the above quality remind us of in regard to humanity's original relationship with God in the Garden of Eden? (p. 51)

17. What is the fourth quality Christ manifested as the Second Adam? (p. 52)

18. Circle one: True or False

    Even if no other men are in agreement with God, God's purposes for the earth can be brought about in Christ. (p. 52)

    Explain your answer: (pp. 52–53)

19. Name the fifth quality Christ manifested as the Second Adam. (p. 53)

20. To review, list three reasons that Christ was able to accomplish our redemption and reclaim our earthly authority. (p. 53)

21. The sixth quality Christ manifested as the Second Adam was that He _____
    _____. (p. 53)

22. Once a person has been redeemed, what is he or she in a position to do? (p. 53)

23. What does God desire to reveal to the visible world through mankind? (p. 53)

24. Circle one: True or False

    The authority Christ transferred to believers is in effect only in regard to our lives on this present earth. (p. 54)

    Explain your answer: (p. 54)

25. For what reasons are many believers not *"having dominion"* in the sense of making a meaningful contribution to furthering the kingdom of God on earth? (pp. 54–55)

26. There are five specific things that our redemption in Christ means for us in regard to our having authority in prayer. What is the first one? (p. 55)

27. Because Christ has delivered us from Satan's dominion, even though we continue to _____ in a fallen world, we do not _____ to it. (p. 56)

28. Now that we belong to God's kingdom, we have _____ over Satan in the _____ of Jesus. (p. 56)

29. What is the second thing our redemption in Christ means for us in regard to authority in prayer? (p. 56)

30. Because of redemption, what now reigns in our lives instead of sin? (p. 56)

31. The third thing our redemption in Christ means for us in regard to authority in prayer is that _____. (p. 56)

32. The fourth thing our redemption in Christ means is that we have _____ to the Father through Jesus' _____. (p. 57)

33. What are two outcomes of this fourth benefit of redemption? (p. 57)

34. Name the fifth thing our redemption in Christ means for us in regard to authority in prayer. (p. 57)

35. Circle one: True or False

    Jesus' name is a magic word we use to get what we want. (p. 57)

    Explain your answer: (p. 57)

36. What is the backbone of prayer composed of? (p. 57)

37. Prayer is joining forces with God the Father by calling attention to His _____. (p. 58)

38. Jesus is not only the One who reclaimed our dominion authority, but He is also our _____ for how we are to live in this authority. (p. 58)

39. Since Jesus was fully divine as well as fully human, did He have an advantage over us in regard to prayer and living for God? Why or why not? (p. 58)

40. How can we model what Jesus did to accomplish God's purposes on the earth? (p. 58)

41. Name the Scripture passage that shows us we can serve God in the same way Jesus did. (p. 59)

42. What will God do for us as we live and work in the Spirit of Christ? (p. 59)

43. What does Christ give us in place of feelings of isolation, uncertainty, and purposelessness that came about as a result of the Fall? (p. 60)

44. After reading this chapter, how would you answer the question, On what basis do you have the right to pray? (p. 59)

Conclusion

Do you want God to bring about His purposes for your life and for our fallen world? You can invite Him to do so through prayer. From Genesis to Revelation, God always found a human being to help Him accomplish His purposes. He comes to you now and asks, in effect, "Are you willing? Will you help Me fulfill My purposes for your life and for the earth? Or are you content to live an unfulfilled existence and to let the influences of sin and Satan encroach upon our world? *'Who is he who will devote himself to be close to me?'* (Jer. 30:21)."

Seek to be close to God, living in oneness with Him and His purposes and exercising the authority He has given you through the Spirit of Christ.

Applying God's Principles to Your Life

Thinking It Over

- Do you feel isolated from God, unsure of where you stand with Him, or unclear about how you should pray? If so, you probably have been praying based on the effects of the Fall rather than on the effects of Christ's work of redemption on your behalf. How will you change the way you approach God based on what you've learned in this chapter?

- Are your prayers based on emotions, feelings, or the theories of men, rather than the Word of God? If so, what will you do to change this pattern?

Praying about It

- Begin today to apply the redemption of Christ to your prayer life by acknowledging Jesus' restoration of your relationship with the Father and your purpose of dominion. Praise God for sending Jesus to earth so that you can have a restored relationship of love with Him, and ask Him to fulfill His purposes in you.

- Before you pray, remind yourself of these promises: *"In [Christ] and through faith in him we may approach God with freedom and confidence"* (Eph. 3:12). *"Let us then approach the throne of grace with confidence, so that we may receive mercy and find grace to help us in our time of need"* (Heb. 4:16).

- Instead of letting your emotions and feelings dominate your prayers, first tell God how you feel, and then continue to pray for the people and circumstances about which you are concerned based on the Word of God and His promises.

Acting on God's Truth

- Have you recognized and accepted your calling and authority in Christ based on the new covenant? When we misunderstand the true nature of humility, we often fail to realize that Christ has truly made us *"a new creation"* (2 Cor. 5:17). Therefore, it is not presumptuous for us to live according to our new nature and authority in Christ. Remind yourself daily that your redemption means that Satan and sin no longer have authority over you, that you have authority and access to the Father through

Jesus' name, and that you have authority through the Word of God.

- The backbone of prayer is our agreement with God's Word, our oneness with Christ, who is the Living Word, and our unity with God's purposes and will. Check your life often to see if you are living in unity with God and His purposes so that your prayers will reflect the same. If you find yourself out of sync with God's ways, yield your life to God again and model Jesus' life: Keep a close relationship with the Father through prayer and do what God directs you to do and what you see Him actively working to accomplish in the world. Rely on the grace and Spirit of God to enable you to obey and serve Him. Remember the covenant God has made with you: *"This is the covenant I will make with the house of Israel after that time,' declares the* LORD. *'I will put my law in their minds and write it on their hearts. I will be their God, and they will be my people'"* (Jer. 31:33).

*"[God] has made us competent as ministers
of a new covenant."*
—2 Corinthians 3:6

Part II
Preparing for Prayer

Chapter Four

How to Enter God's Presence

*We must learn to enter God's presence with the right spirit,
approach, and preparation so we can commune with Him
and offer effective prayers as God's priests.*

CHAPTER THEME

Once we understand that the heart of prayer is communion with God in a unity of love and purpose, how do we begin to pray? Where do we start? We first need to learn how to enter God's presence with the right spirit, approach, and preparation so that we can have this communion with Him.

We will do so by seeing how the New Testament principle of "the priesthood of believers" is illustrated by the practices of the high priest in the Old Testament. The New Testament reveals the deeper spiritual meanings of Old Testament ways and rituals, which were fulfilled in Jesus Christ. It is important to understand these Old Testament practices so we can appreciate what their fulfillment in the New Testament means for our relationship with God now that we are redeemed in Christ.

Questions for Reflection

1. What do you think it means to "enter into God's presence"?

2. Do you prepare for worship and prayer in any way? Why or why not?

Exploring God's Principles and Purposes

3. Many Christians today fail to fully enter into God's presence because— [choose one] (p. 65)

    (a) they don't sing enough songs beforehand.

    (b) they often do not have a genuine reverence for God.

    (c) they don't use the right words when praying.

    (d) God doesn't want to interact with them.

4. Have you noticed a lack of true respect for God in the twenty-first century church? If so, in what ways?

5. Why are many of today's Christians casual in their obedience to God? (p. 66)

6. Rather than canceling God's law, what is the true nature and role of grace? (p. 66)

7. What effect can an apathetic attitude toward God have on our prayers? (p. 66)

8. What should our motivation for obeying God be? (p. 66)

9. Why is holiness critical to prayer? (p. 67)

10. What does it mean to *"see"* God in the sense given in Hebrews 12:14 and Matthew 5:8? (p. 67)

11. What does the word *holy* mean? (p. 67)

12. Based on the above definition, what does it mean to be pure or holy in heart? (p. 67)

13. Why does God say we are to be holy? (p. 68)

14. In what way are we to be "separated" in holiness? (p. 68)

15. Why is holiness the key both to being persistent in prayer and receiving answers to prayer? (p. 68)

16. In what sense is a person who is double-minded demonstrating a lack of holiness? (pp. 68–69)

17. Complete the following: When we go to God in prayer, we must have the same _____ between what we _____ and _____ that He does, because holiness is _____ the truth and then _____ the truth. (p. 69)

18. When we pray according to God's Word and promises, yet are double-minded, what happens to these prayers? (p. 69)

19. On what basis can we trust God to fulfill what He has promised? (p. 70)

20. From the creation of the world, what role has God always desired that people fulfill? What is the nature of this role? (pp. 71–72)

21. When humanity rebelled against God and continually failed in this role, how did God restore this purpose to mankind? (p. 72)

22. What Scripture shows us that the role of priesthood has been restored to mankind through the church? (p. 73)

23. In light of questions nine through nineteen regarding holiness, why do you think the priesthood of believers is described as a "holy" priesthood?

24. God's intention through Christ was to create a new nation (the church) in which everybody would receive the _____ _____, through whom they could be God's intermediaries for the world. (p. 74)

25. There are ten steps through which we are to prepare to enter the presence of God so we will be able to commune with Him, offer effectual prayer, and be His mediators on behalf of the world. What is the first step? (p. 75)

26. If we desire to enter God's presence, what has to be dealt with first? (p. 75)

27. How are we to deal with them? (p. 76)

28. What Scripture tells us that our sins keep God from hearing our prayers? (p. 76)

29. What brings the power of agreement in prayer? (p. 77)

30. What is the second step to entering God's presence? (p. 77)

31. This step corresponds to what New Testament admonition? (p. 77)

32. Through whose righteousness alone are we able to come before God? How do we live in this righteousness on a daily basis? (p. 79)

33. The third step to entering God's presence is to
_____.
(p. 79)

34. God desires that we give more than the appearance of truth. According to Psalm 51:6, He desires truth in the "_____ *parts*" of our lives. (p. 79)

35. Define these parts of our lives. (p. 79)

36. How can we be pure before God in our inner parts? (p. 80)

37. The fourth step to entering God's presence is to _____ with the _____. (p. 80)

38. What does it mean for us to be in the Word when we come before God? (p. 81)

39. The Word will purify our _____ and _____. (p. 81)

40. What is the fifth step to entering God's presence? (p. 81)

41. In John 4:23–24, Jesus said that true worshippers worship God in what way? (p. 82)

42. What do you think it means to worship in the above way?

43. Name the sixth step to entering God's presence. (p. 82)

44. From what do we need to separate ourselves when preparing for prayer? (p. 82)

45. Where is the "place" in which we meet God? How can we meet Him there? (p. 83)

46. What is one thing we can do to help us reach this "place"? (p. 83)

47. How does doing this thing help us to reach God? (p. 83)

48. The seventh step to entering God's presence is to
_____. (p. 83)

49. How does Dr. Munroe define this step? (p. 83)

50. Hebrews 4:16 says that we can *"come boldly to the throne of grace"* (NKJV). On what basis can we enter boldly where God dwells? (p. 86)

51. What is the eighth step to entering God's presence? (p. 86)

52. When we give God the glory, what are we confessing to Him? (p. 86)

53. What are we to do with the "glory" or excess that God has blessed us with? [choose one] (p. 86)

    (a) hoard it

    (b) spend it on whatever we want

    (c) gamble with it

    (d) give it back to God so that others who have needs can be blessed

54. Name the ninth step to entering God's presence. (p. 87)

55. Why do we need to wash in the Word when we've already been cleansed by it? (p. 87)

56. How do we wash in the Word? (p. 87)

57. What is the tenth step to entering God's presence? (p. 87)

58. How can we fulfill this step? (p. 87)

59. How did Christ enable us to live in a state of continual union with God? (p. 87)

Conclusion

We need to remain in a state of preparedness for prayer by living out the ten steps to entering God's presence. God is a God of holiness, and we aren't to approach Him in an offhand or careless way. It is important that we learn what it means to honor the Lord and to reflect His nature and character in our lives. We must always remember that Jesus Christ has made it possible for us to fulfill each of these steps of preparation for prayer. It is because of Christ alone that we can enter the presence of an almighty and holy God and call Him *"Abba, Father"* (Rom. 8:15).

Applying God's Principles to Your Life

Thinking It Over

• Do you have true reverence for God? How can you better honor Him in your heart and life?

- Are you being casual about your sins, without regard for God's holiness? If so, what will you do to take sin more seriously and repent of it?

- Have you been approaching God on the basis of Christ's sacrifice alone, or are you trying to get God to accept you by doing good deeds and being a "good" person? What have you learned in this chapter about the nature of Christ's atonement for you?

- In what state of heart do you normally go to God in prayer? What area(s) of preparedness for prayer do you most need to work on?

- What does it mean to you that you are a member of the priesthood of believers?

Praying about It

- If you have been apathetic about sin in your life, ask God to forgive you and to search your heart to show you specific sins for which you need to repent. Accept Christ's forgiveness and cleansing, and ask Him to fill you with His Spirit so you can live for Him.

- Before you pray, review the ten steps of preparedness for entering God's presence. See what steps you may be omitting and which areas you need to set right before God. Fulfill those steps today.

- Develop an attitude of praise and worship toward God, keeping in mind that He wants us to worship Him *"in spirit and in truth"* (John 4:24).

Acting on God's Truth

- God tells us, *"You will seek me and find me when you seek me with all your heart"* (Jer. 29:13). Below, write down at least three ways you can better seek God with all your heart:

- David expressed to God, *"Surely you desire truth in the inner parts"* (Ps. 51:6). The *"inner parts"* are the areas of our lives that only we know about. Are you living in integrity in your innermost being? List several areas of your inner life that you need to put right with God. Ask God to forgive you for not living in truth in these areas, and to enable you to live in integrity in your inward thoughts and desires as well as your outward actions.

- Meditate on your role as "priest" before God on behalf of the world. Then, let that perspective guide your daily prayers.

"True worshipers will worship the Father
in spirit and truth."
—John 4:23

Chapter Five

Cultivating the God Kind of Faith

There is positive faith and there is negative faith. Both come by the same means—by what we listen to and believe.

CHAPTER THEME

In the previous chapter, we learned what it means to prepare our hearts to enter God's presence so we can eliminate obstacles to unanswered prayer and be effective in God's purposes. This chapter examines another reason why our prayers may fail to work: We often have the wrong kind of faith. Understanding the different kinds of faith, and how faith functions, are key preparations for prayer.

Questions for Reflection

1. What has God promised in His Word that you have the most difficulty believing? Why?

2. What is one thing that you believe, beyond any doubt, will happen in your life? Why do you believe this?

Exploring God's Principles and Purposes

3. Circle one: True or False

    Everyone lives by faith. (p. 91)

    Explain your answer: (p. 91)

4. Why must we be able to function in the faith the Bible speaks of? (p. 91)

5. In general terms, what does it mean to have faith? (p. 92)

6. How does God Himself operate? (p. 92)

7. Since we were created to operate in the same way God does, what does God's method of creating the world teach us about the way we are to pray? (pp. 92–93)

8. Complete the following: What you say is a reflection of what is in your _____, of what you _____. (p. 93)

9. Why is it true that we will likely *have* what we *say* the most? (p. 93)

10. Faith is belief combined with _____ and _____. (p. 94)

11. What is one reason God sometimes doesn't answer our prayers? (p. 94)

12. What is the literal translation of Jesus' statement *"Have faith in God"* (Mark 11:22)? (p. 95)

13. Circle one: True or False

    When Romans 10:17 says, *"Faith comes by hearing"* (NKJV), it is saying that faith only initially comes by hearing. (p. 96)

    Explain your answer: (p. 96)

14. You will become what you _____ to and speak what you _____. (p. 96)

15. Where does the God kind of faith come from? (pp. 96–97)

16. If you have filled your heart and mind with the Word of God, what will this do for you in times of trouble and adversity? (p. 97)

17. You can be _____ or _____ affected by what you say and believe. (p. 98)

18. If you pray for something, then start saying the opposite, what can happen? (p. 98)

19. When you pray about something, what are the conditions under which you won't be ashamed concerning it? (pp. 99–100)

20. Why is it important to spend time with other people of faith? (p. 100)

21. What will happen if we stay connected to the Word of God—God's truth? (p. 101)

22. When we trust in God, believe His promises, and see the answers to our prayers, what effect will we have on others? (p. 102)

23. Since faith, active belief, and expectation all come by what we hear, what is the foremost source we should be listening to? (p. 102)

24. What have we been trained to think about "reality"? (pp. 102–3)

25. Why is a person who is *not* living in the faith of God not living in reality? (p. 103)

26. What is Satan's goal in terms of our faith? (p. 104)

27. How should we respond when we hear words that are contrary to God's Word? (pp. 103–4)

Conclusion

Unanswered prayer can have more to do with our having the wrong *kind* of faith than a *lack* of faith. There is positive faith and there is negative faith, and both come by the same means. They come by what we listen to and believe. The God kind of faith comes from *"hearing"* God's Word (Rom. 10:17)—listening to it, reading it, and believing it. We need to immerse ourselves in the Word of God so that it will flow continuously into our lives and our prayers will bear fruit in season.

Applying God's Principles to Your Life

Thinking It Over

- How much time do you spend in God's Word compared to taking in other perspectives from television, movies, books, magazines, the Internet, and even other people? What does your answer indicate about the ideas and thoughts you value most?

- Which influences you most—God's Word or what others say? Why?

- If faith is belief in action, what do your actions say about what you believe?

- What is the first thing you think or say when trouble or problems come into your life? How does this reflect what is in your heart?

- Overall, are the words you speak having a positive or negative effect on your life? In what ways?

- Are there people in your life who are more influential on you in a negative way than you are on them in a positive way? If so, how will you respond to this situation?

Praying about It

- What kind of faith are you bringing to your prayers? Pray that God will help you place your trust in Him and

His Word rather than in the words of faith around you that are contrary to His truth. Ask for His forgiveness if you have spent more time dwelling on your own plans, ideas, and analyses rather than on taking His Word into your heart and living by it. Ask Him to open the truths of His Word to you and enable you to rely on Him alone.

- Have you been tempted to give up on something that you are praying for? Make sure your prayer is based on God's will and Word, and then keep on praying and believing that God will answer it in its own season.

Acting on God's Truth

- List examples of positive faith and negative faith in your life:

- The God kind of faith puts its full trust in God's Word. What will you do to give yourself a constant diet of the Word of God, so that it will fill your heart and mind and become the basis of your life and prayers?

- Since other kinds of faith besides the God kind of faith are all around you, check what you're listening to and whom you're listening to: the company you're keeping, the books you're reading, the music you're listening to, the movies and videos you're watching, even the church you're attending. Make sure you are filling your life with faith in God's Word. Plant yourself in a place where the Word is prevalent and the people around you are continually speaking and living it. If your spouse and children are negative, live in a way that expresses your own faith and speak the Word of God to them as you have opportunity.

- During the day, list any negative thoughts you think or that others say to you. In the evening, review them and counteract them with what God says in His Word.

- Start developing the God kind of faith by taking one situation in your life and finding out what God's Word says about it. Write down your findings, pray about the situation in light of them, and hold fast to the Word whenever you are tempted to doubt.

"Faith comes by hearing, and hearing by the word of God."
—Romans 10:17 NKJV

Part III
Principles of Prayer

Chapter Six
Jesus' Model Prayer

*The secret to Jesus' success in ministry was
a lifestyle of prayer.*

CHAPTER THEME

Jesus' disciples lived with Him for three and a half years. They went everywhere He went and saw all the things He did. Yet the Bible records only one thing they asked Him to teach them, and that was how to pray (Luke 11:1). We might wonder, "Why would the disciples ask to learn to pray rather than to do the 'big things' like feeding multitudes, calming storms, casting out demons, healing the sick, raising the dead, or walking on water?" It is because they saw Jesus pray more than anything else. The secret to Jesus' success in ministry was a lifestyle of prayer.

Question for Reflection

1. What do you think of Martin Luther's observation that "more work is done by prayer than by work itself"?

Exploring God's Principles and Purposes

2. Why did Jesus' disciples conclude that the prayers Jesus prayed were more important than the other things—even miracles—that He did during the day? (pp. 109–10)

3. Circle one: True or False

   We can never really be too busy to pray. (p. 110)

4. Through prayer— [choose one] (pp. 110–11)

   (a) our lives are much more focused, efficient, and peaceful.

   (b) we receive wisdom and guidance to address our problems and concerns.

   (c) we are prevented from doing things through trial and error.

   (d) God tells us what is really important, compared to what seems urgent.

   (e) we can make every act count.

   (f) we are enabled to think clearly and wisely.

   (g) we receive discernment we wouldn't otherwise have.

   (f) all of the above

5. What did Jesus explain was the result of His intimacy with the Father in prayer? (pp. 111–12) [See also John 5:17, 19–20.]

6. How does Jesus' pattern of going to the Father and doing what the Father revealed to Him relate to what we've learned about the nature and purpose of prayer? (p. 112)

7. Why did Jesus spend hours in prayer? (p. 113)

8. We often spend hours discussing national problems with others without coming up with any solutions. Yet what often happens when we spend time in prayer about these problems? (p. 113)

9. Ninety-nine percent of the time, God speaks to us in what way? [choose one] (p. 114)

    (a) to our minds, through our spirits

    (b) through angels

    (c) through miraculous signs

    (d) through prophets

10. Why does God speak in this way? (p. 114)

11. In what ways did Dr. Munroe say God has spoken to him in his mind and spirit, indicating the various ways God may speak to us? (p. 115)

12. Complete the following sentences:

    Prayer is a personal and private _____ and _____. (p. 117)

    _____ prayer should never be a substitute for personal and private time with the Father. (p. 117)

13. Circle one: True or False

    Prayer is just "talking to God." (p. 117)

14. Circle one: True or False

    Prayer is not automatic, but rather a function that must be taught. (p. 117)

15. What we know as "The Lord's Prayer" is a _____ for prayer rather than words we need to repeat exactly. (p. 118)

16. Christ taught us to pray in order to enable us to fulfill what purpose? (p. 118)

17. In Jesus' model prayer, found in Luke 11:2–4 (NKJV), what is the significance of the phrase *"**Our** Father"* (emphasis added)? (pp. 118–19)

18. What is one reason we are to address God as *"Father"*? (p. 119)

19. When we acknowledge that God is *"in heaven,"* what two things are we confessing? (p. 119)

20. Why did Jesus teach us to pray, *"Hallowed be Your name?"* (pp. 119–20)

21. What is the significance of our praying this concept: *"Your kingdom come. Your will be done on earth as it is in heaven"*? (p. 120)

22. As we align ourselves with God's will, and pray in love and compassion for God's will to be done in others' lives, what will God do for us? (pp. 120–21)

23. When we pray for daily needs, why are we to pray using the plural, *"Give **us** day by day our daily bread"* (emphasis added)? (p. 121)

24. What does the term *"daily bread"* refer to? (pp. 121–22)

25. Why did Jesus teach us to pray, *"And forgive us our sins, for we also forgive everyone who is indebted to us"*? (pp. 122–23)

26. Having good _____ is one of the keys to answered prayer. (p. 122)

27. Why is love just as important an element of answered prayer as faith is? (p. 123)

28. When we ask God not to *"lead us into temptation, but deliver us from the evil one,"* does this statement imply that God might deliberately steer us toward temptation? (p. 124)

29. What can we do to protect ourselves from temptation? (p. 124)

30. What is the significance of completing our prayers with this thought: *"For Yours is the kingdom and the power and the glory forever. Amen"*? (pp. 124–25)

Conclusion

Jesus wants us to operate in the way He operated when He was on earth: with much time in communion and love with the Father, and much accomplished for the kingdom. Your prayer life can make you so intimate with God that you will naturally manifest the works, or thoughts, of God, just as Jesus did.

The entire book of Acts describes how the disciples continued the ministry of Jesus through prayer and the power of the Holy Spirit. They learned the secret to Jesus' effectiveness in ministry. Now that you have learned the same secret, what will you do with it?

Applying God's Principles to Your Life

Thinking It Over

- Have you ever felt you were "too busy" to pray? If so, how has your perspective on this changed since reading this chapter?

- How would you describe your relationship with the heavenly Father? Intimate? Loving? Guarded? Distant? How does your relationship with God differ from Christ's, and what can you do to make it more similar?

- Are your prayers heartfelt expressions of communion with God—or more like shopping lists or rote repetition? What have you learned in this chapter about the nature of true prayer?

- Do you include others in your prayers, or are your prayers focused mainly on yourself? How do you think your life will change if you pray for others more?

Praying about It

- Jesus spent hours in prayer because He had a genuine relationship with the Father, and any relationship takes time to build and maintain. We, also, are called to a lifestyle of prayer. Ask God to fulfill that calling in you. Pray that He will give you a heart to seek an intimate relationship with Him every day and to follow His thoughts and ways rather than your own thoughts and ways—or others' opinions.

• Since broken relationships often keep our prayers from being answered, set aside a time to pray and fast, and ask God to reveal the hurt, bitterness, and anger you are holding against people. Yield to the conviction of the Holy Spirit and freely forgive those who have wronged you, drawing on the love and strength of Christ to help you do so. Also, freely forgive others who are holding grudges against you. Then you will be able to live in love and forgiveness and experience true fellowship with your heavenly Father. Although forgiving others may seem difficult at first, don't give up. Allow God to fill your heart with His love and grace as you yield to Him.

• After taking the above step, make it a practice, each day, to ask yourself if there is anyone in your family, local church, job, and so on with whom you aren't in good relationship. Then ask God to give you the grace to forgive anyone against whom you are bitter or resentful.

• When you pray, make sure you include prayers for the needs of others, and the purposes of the kingdom of heaven, and not just your own needs and desires. Ask God to give you love and compassion for others that will overflow into your prayers.

Acting on God's Truth

• Read the book of John, making special note of any time Jesus talked about His work, His relationship with the Father, and the love the Father has for Him. Ask God to enable you to develop the intimate relationship with Him that Jesus had—and has.

• Use Jesus' model prayer as a guideline for your daily prayers. Take each step and personalize it so that it is a heartfelt expression of your growing relationship with

God. Remember that you don't need to repeat the words *exactly,* but instead should use them as a pattern for your prayers.

- Over the next few weeks, increase the time you spend with God in prayer each day in order to build and maintain a relationship of intimacy with Him.

- Do a Bible study on the nature and purposes of God's kingdom so you can pray, *"Your kingdom come. Your will be done on earth as it is in heaven,"* with more knowledge, wisdom, and conviction.

Hours with God make minutes with men effective.

Chapter Seven

Twelve Action Steps to Prayer

Proven principles of prayer from biblical figures whose prayers were powerful and effective.

CHAPTER THEME

This chapter provides a useful approach for organizing your steps in prayer. The principles outlined were developed from Dr. Munroe's evaluation of the prayer lives of Jesus, Abraham, Joseph, Moses, David, Ezekiel, and others in the Bible, who all used a similar pattern in prayer. Their prayers received the attention of God and produced powerful results.

Question for Reflection

1. What elements do you include in your prayers (e.g., worship, petition, thanksgiving)? Are there any elements you feel you have been neglecting? If so, what are they?

Exploring God's Principles and Purposes

2. This chapter summarizes "twelve actions steps" that will help make our prayers more powerful and effective. What is the first step, and how is it defined? (pp. 129–30)

3. How can we accomplish this step? (p. 129)

4. What definition of prayer reflects our need to put aside all else so we can *"be still, and know that* [He is] *God"* (Ps. 46:10)? (p. 130)

5. What happens when we try to pray, but our spirits, bodies, minds, and emotions are not unified? (pp. 130–31)

6. Complete the following: Silence helps bring you into a unity of _____ and _____ with yourself and God. (p. 131)

7. What is the second action step to prayer? (p. 131)

8. In what way are we to worship God? (p. 131)

9. The third action step to prayer is to _____ _____ (p. 132)

10. Rather than being an emotional response to our sins and failures, what is the true meaning of confession? (p. 132)

11. How does adoration prepare the way for confession? (p. 132)

12. Circle one: True or False

    When God deals with us about our sin and rebellion against Him, we are to feel condemned. (p. 132)

    Explain your answer: (pp. 132–33)

13. Unforgiven sin is sin that you never _____ as sin. You keep _____ onto it and _____ it; therefore, God cannot cleanse you from it. (p. 133)

14. What can happen when we continue to play with sin and don't agree with God about it? (p. 135)

15. Once God cleanses you, there isn't anyone who can _____ you. (p. 136) [See Romans 8:33–34.]

16. What is the fourth action step to prayer? (p. 136)

17. Why are we better able to offer thanks and praise to God after we have confessed? (p. 136)

18. The fifth action step to prayer is to _____ _____. (p. 136)

19. What does it mean to offer supplication? (pp. 136–37)

20. Why is supplication usually a natural outgrowth of giving thanks? (p. 137)

21. Name the sixth action step to prayer. (p. 137)

22. Prayer is a very articulate, _____ communication. (p. 137)

23. When we petition God for things we want Him to do, we have to be sure the _____ we bring is _____ to the case. (p. 137)

24. In what ways can we address God specifically and intentionally? (pp. 137–38)

25. What is the seventh action step to prayer? (p. 138)

26. What does this step involve? (p. 138)

27. The eighth action step to prayer is to _____. (p. 140)

28. Circle one: True or False

    Pleading our case means begging and moaning before God until He feels sorry for us enough to answer our prayers. (p. 140)

29. In the parable of the unjust judge, why did Jesus use the most severe example of a source of help to represent God? (p. 140)

30. In the same parable, why did Jesus use the worst-case scenario—a destitute widow—to represent the one who is praying? (p. 141)

31. We need to hold on to God's promises because He will give _____ to His chosen ones, those who have received His _____ as a spiritual _____. (p. 142)

32. What is the ninth action step to prayer? (p. 142)

33. When we ask God for something according to His Word, what should our attitude be concerning our request? (p. 143)

34. We usually give up too soon when we don't see immediate answers to our prayers, but what will happen if we have the above perspective? (p. 143)

35. The tenth action step to prayer is to _____ _____. (p. 143)

36. What is the difference between the first and second "thanksgivings" (the difference between step four and step ten)? (pp. 143–44)

37. We are not to wait until we see the _____ of our answers before expressing our _____. (p. 144)

38. Name the eleventh action step to prayer. (p. 145)

39. How do we fulfill this step? (p. 145)

40. The twelfth action step to prayer is to _____
_____. (p. 146)

41. What Scripture illustrates this step? (p. 146)

42. What does it mean for us to actively believe? (p. 146)

Conclusion

As we learn how to pray according to biblical principles, we will become powerfully effective believers. Use these twelve action steps as a guide for your prayers, and make sure everything in your life is in order according to God's will and purposes. Then watch what God does in your life as you grow in the grace and knowledge of God and His ways and continue to live before Him in holiness and truth.

Applying God's Principles to Your Life

Thinking It Over

- Do you take the time to quiet yourself before the Lord prior to prayer, or do you usually pray hurriedly, treating prayer as just one more task in your day? What are the benefits of "being still and knowing that the Lord is God"? (See Psalm 46:10.)

- What causes you to become distracted when you pray? What can you do to eliminate those distractions?

- Do you pray sporadically and haphazardly, or do you pray purposefully according to God's Word? How will you change your approach to prayer based on what you have learned in this chapter?

Praying about It

- Begin your prayer times by letting the Lord calm your heart in the midst of the problems, demands, and distractions of your life. Remember that God *"will keep in perfect peace him whose mind is steadfast, because he trusts in* [God]*"* (Isa. 26:3).

- Give adoration to God for who He is. Use Dr. Munroe's examples on pp. 131–32 as a basis for your worship.

- If you have been justifying any wrongdoing in your life, make confession before God by agreeing with Him that it is sin. Truly repent by turning from your sin and asking God to cleanse you from all unrighteousness. (See 1 John 1:9.)

- Make it a practice to offer two kinds of thanksgiving to God: thanksgiving for His mercy, and thanksgiving for His having already answered the requests you have made.

Acting on God's Truth

- This week, gradually begin incorporating all twelve action steps into your prayers.

- Practice specifying your petitions by acknowledging both God's name and His Word. For example, in regard to His name, if you seek peace, appeal to Him as Jehovah-Shalom (The Lord our Peace); if you need provision, pray to Him as Jehovah-Jireh (The Lord our Provider); if you desire healing, go to Him as Jehovah-Rapha (The Lord our Healer).

  In regard to His Word, write down what you want to pray for. Next to those items, write down the relevant Scriptures that you will present to God when you pray. Then, when you pray about your list of petitions, God will know that there is thought and intention behind your requests as you pray according to His Word.

- Take one thing you are praying for, start living in expectation of it, and practice active belief by making arrangements for receiving the answer.

"The prayer of a righteous man is powerful and effective."
—James 5:16

Chapter Eight

Hurdles to Answered Prayer

Recognizing and overcoming hurdles to answered prayer will protect your prayer potential and give you the right motivation and perspective for prayer.

CHAPTER THEME

Satan recognizes the power of true prayer to bring the kingdom of God on earth. Therefore, he makes it his business to try to cause the prayers of individuals and churches to be ineffective. He will use misconceptions about prayer to thwart our prayer potential. These misconceptions are hurdles to overcome as we address the problems that lead to unanswered prayer. This chapter clearly delineates a number of mistaken beliefs about prayer so we can see how they differ from the definition of prayer that is based on the Word of God. When we rise above these hurdles through God's grace, we will truly understand the purpose and power of prayer.

Questions for Reflection

1. What do you think is the greatest misconception about prayer in the church today? Why do you think this?

2. What is one misconception about prayer that you used to have? How did you recognize and overcome it, and what difference has overcoming it made in your prayer life?

Exploring God's Principles and Purposes

3. What is the first hurdle to answered prayer? (p. 151)

4. Complete the following: We often have the _____ idea that if we _____ a great deal about prayer, somehow we *have* prayed. (p. 152)

5. If we don't apply the principles of prayer to our lives, our _____ won't help us _____. (p. 152)

6. What is the best approach to prayer? (p. 152)

7. The second hurdle to answered prayer is _____ _____. (p. 152)

8. How does the above differ from true faith? (p. 152)

9. The true believer is a _____ of the Word and not a _____ only (James 1:23). (p. 153)

10. What is a variation of mental assent, and why is it a hurdle for us? (p. 153)

11. Why has sense knowledge become one of the biggest obstacles to faith in many cultures? (p. 153)

12. According to James 1:22, if we think listening to the Word, by itself, will make a difference in our lives, we are _____ ourselves. (p. 154)

13. Name the third hurdle to answered prayer. (p. 155)

14. What happens when we fail to absorb God's Word into our lives? (p. 155)

15. According to James 1:25, what will happen if we both remember God's Word and put it into practice in our lives? (p. 156)

16. How are we to absorb the Word? (p. 156)

17. Describe the nature of biblical meditation. (pp. 156–57)

18. If we allow Satan to steal the Word from us because we haven't let it become part of our lives, what else can he steal from us? (pp. 157–58)

19. When the Word becomes a part of our lives, why can't the devil stop it from being effective? (p. 158)

20. What is the fourth hurdle to answered prayer? (p. 158)

21. In what two ways can our views about hope interfere with what God wants to accomplish through prayer? (p. 158)

22. What is the difference between biblical faith and biblical hope? (p. 158)

23. How does the misapplication of biblical hope become a hurdle to answered prayer? (p. 159)

24. When we exhibit wishful thinking rather than faith, we show that— [choose one] (pp. 160–61)

    (a) we don't trust God.

    (b) we don't believe God.

    (c) we are skeptical about God's character and integrity.

    (d) all of the above

25. What is the result of wishful thinking? (p. 161)

26. The fifth hurdle to answered prayer is _____ _____. (p. 161)

27. Why did Dr. Munroe say we shouldn't pray for faith? (p. 161)

28. How, then, does faith grow? (p. 161)

29. Circle one: True or False

    We don't need to ask God for more faith, but to use the faith we already have. (p. 161)

30. It is not the size of our faith that counts—it is the size of our _____. (p. 162)

31. If we want to build our faith, what should we do? (p. 162)

32. What is the sixth hurdle to answered prayer, and what does it involve? (p. 162)

33. What will happen to the person who doesn't regard prayer as important or who allows life to crowd out his practice of prayer? (p. 162)

Conclusion

We must be careful not to become complacent in our knowledge of the Word and neglect to nurture it in our lives. However, when we hear, absorb, and apply the Word, we will bear the fruit of much spiritual growth and answered prayer. We will see some of God's original purposes for blessing the earth fulfilled through our very lives.

Applying God's Principles to Your Life

Thinking It Over

- Which of the hurdles in this chapter best describes your current practice of praying and reading the Bible? What attitude or outlook do you need to repent of in order to rise above this hurdle through God's grace?

- Mental assent *agrees* with God but does not *believe* God. Think of a favorite Scripture that you enjoy reading but which, deep down, you don't really believe. (This process might seem uncomfortable at first, but will be well worth the effort.) Then turn your knowledge of that Scripture into true faith in His Word.

- Have you been treating faith and hope as if they were merely wishful thinking? What have you learned in this chapter about how wishful thinking differs from true biblical faith and hope? How has your perspective changed based on what you have learned?

Praying about It

- Pray that God's Holy Spirit would show you where you are being deceived in your attitudes toward prayer and the Word so you can understand and practice true and effective prayer. Ask Him to help you remain alert to the hurdles in your life that the enemy wants to use to destroy your prayer potential. Resist the enemy as you stand firm in your faith. (See 1 Peter 1:8–9.)

- Each day, as you read the Bible, ask God to open the eyes of your heart to see what He is saying to you through His Word. Meditate on the Word by spending time thinking about the implications and applications of what you have read, and then immediately put it into practice in your life.

- Do you tend to be an "I'll believe it when I see it" person? While this outlook may be appropriate in some situations, when it comes to believing God's Word, it can undermine your faith. The answers to our prayers often won't become a manifested reality in our lives until we believe they are real before we see them—through fully trusting God and His Word. What are you skeptical of in God's Word? Ask God to lead you on the path to believing His Word. *"Faith is being sure of what we hope for and certain of what we do not see"* (Heb. 11:1).

Acting on God's Truth

- We gain a false sense of satisfaction when we learn *about* something, but don't actually *do* it. Think about one area of your life in which you are being a hearer only and not a doer in regard to the teaching of God's Word. (See James 1:23.) Purpose to obey or put into practice that command or truth from Scripture today. Every time you read the Word or hear good teaching and put it into practice, your spiritual life will be strengthened a little more.

- Do you wish you had more faith? The Bible says that faith comes by hearing the Word of God. (See Romans 10:17.) Make daily Bible reading and regular study of the Scriptures a part of your life. When you continually receive the Word into your mind and spirit, your faith will grow.

- After church this week, spend at least five minutes sitting quietly, reflecting on the message and what God is saying to you through it. Think about how you can apply it to your life.

"Be self-controlled and alert. Your enemy the devil prowls around like a roaring lion looking for someone to devour. Resist him, standing firm in the faith."
—1 Peter 5:8–9

Chapter Nine
Hindrances to Answered Prayer

Clearing out hindrances in our lives will enable us to
live in harmony with God and others and to have
confidence in prayer.

CHAPTER THEME

I n addition to the hurdles described in the last chapter,
there are spiritual and emotional hindrances to prayer
that we need to address if we are to have true fellowship
with God and receive answers to our prayers. When we can
recognize and understand the major obstacles that hinder
our prayers, we can more effectively deal with them.

Question for Reflection

1. What do you think is the major hindrance to your
   prayers being answered?

Exploring God's Principles and Purposes

2. What is the first major hindrance to answered prayer? (p. 165)

3. What do Isaiah 59:1 and Psalm 66:18 say are the results of iniquity in our lives? (pp. 165–66)

4. What does John 3:22 say is the reason we receive what we ask of God? (p. 166)

5. What should we do if we have sinned? (p. 166)

6. What is the second major hindrance to answered prayer? (p. 166)

7. How does this hindrance affect our prayers? (p. 166)

8. Complete the following: Fear is believing what the _____ is telling you and what _____ _____ are telling you rather than what _____ is saying to you. (p. 166)

9. On what basis can we go to God in prayer even when we have sinned or feel we have failed God? (pp. 166–67)

10. The third major hindrance to unanswered prayer is _____. (p. 167)

11. What Scripture assures us that we don't have to go around with a constant sense of being condemned by God? (pp. 167–68)

12. Sometimes guilt comes from _____ that God has forgiven us for our sin. (p. 168)

13. How does the enemy use guilt against us? (p. 168)

14. Isaiah 43:25 says that God— [choose one] (p. 169)

    (a) is indifferent toward our sin.

    (b) blots out our transgressions and doesn't remember our sins.

    (c) refuses to forgive us even when we confess our sins to Him.

    (d) forgives small sins but not the larger ones.

15. Name the fourth hindrance to answered prayer and what often causes this hindrance in people's lives. (p. 170)

16. What does Ephesians 1:4–11 tells us about how God truly feels about us? (p. 170)

17. A low opinion of yourself or self-hatred is not from God, but from the _____. He doesn't want us to know that our value to God is _____ (p. 171)

18. In light of our value to God, how should we treat ourselves, and how should we approach God in prayer? (p. 171)

19. What is the fifth major hindrance to answered prayer? (p. 174)

20. What does James 1:8 say about the person who doubts? (p. 174)

21. What action shows that we believe God will answer our prayers? (pp. 174–75)

22. _____ _____ is the sixth significant hindrance to answered prayer. (p. 175)

23. What are some wrong motives that can encroach on our prayers? (p. 175)

24. What should be our motivation in prayer? (p. 175)

25. Circle one: True or False

    It is wrong for us to ask God to meet our needs. (p. 175)

26. On what basis does God say He will supply our daily needs? (pp. 175–76)

27. What is the seventh major hindrance to answered prayer? (p. 176)

28. What does it mean to be bitter? (p. 176)

29. What general effect does bitterness have on us? (pp. 176–77)

30. In what way does bitterness affect our prayers? (p. 176)

31. How can we guard against bitterness? (p. 177)

32. The eighth significant hindrance to answered prayer is _____. (p. 177)

33. How does this hindrance impede our prayers, and in what two ways does it do this? (pp. 177–78)

34. What is the ninth major hindrance to answered prayer? (p. 178)

35. How does this hindrance negatively affect our prayers? (p. 178)

36. What should we do to address this hindrance? (pp. 178–79)

37. Name the tenth significant hindrance to answered prayer. (p. 179)

38. What is an "idol of the heart"? (p. 179)

39. What place does God deserve in our lives? (p. 179)

40. The eleventh hindrance to answered prayer is _____. (p. 179)

41. What Scripture emphasizes this truth, and what does this passage imply? (p. 179)

42. What Scriptures promise us that if we are compassionate and generous to our fellowmen and give to God willingly, we can be assured that our prayers will be answered? (p. 180)

Conclusion

Hebrews 12:1 says, *"Let us throw off ["lay aside" NKJV] everything that hinders and the sin that so easily entangles, and let us run with perseverance the race marked out for us."* When we remove hindrances to answered prayer from our lives, we will be able to live in harmony with God and others, and have confidence and effectiveness in prayer.

Applying God's Principles to Your Life

Thinking It Over

•   Is there anything in your life that is keeping you from a clear conscience and unbroken fellowship with God? If so, what is it?

- Have you confessed your sins to God and asked for His forgiveness? Have you accepted the forgiveness of God, or are you still holding on to past sins and guilt?

- Have you truly recognized that you are a child of God? Meditate on your value to God based on Luke 15:11–24; Ephesians 1:4–11; Hebrews 10.

- Have you been asking God for something in order to promote your own ego or for other selfish purposes? Or have you been asking God to fulfill His Word so that His kingdom can come on the earth?

- Are you harboring bitterness or unforgiveness against anyone? If so, who is it? What will you do about the situation, based on what you have learned in this chapter about the connection between forgiveness and answered prayer?

Praying about It

- When you pray, keep in mind who you are in Christ and what God has promised you. If you do not immediately receive an answer to your prayers, be careful not to allow feelings of unworthiness or impatience to cause you to think God cannot or will not answer. Your prayer has been answered and will be manifested in God's time.

- If there are relationships in your life that need mending, ask God to help you let go of any bitterness you may have. Take a step this week to repair at least one of these relationships by forgiving someone or asking for forgiveness.

Acting on God's Truth

- Christ has already made you perfect in Him through His sacrifice on the cross, yet you are also in a process of *"being made holy"* (Heb. 10:14). If you have known sin in your life, put it under the blood of Jesus. Let Him cast your sin in that sea of forgetfulness so that you can have power in prayer with God. Seek reconciliation in your broken relationships and restitution for wrongs you have committed, as God leads. If you sin in the future, ask God to forgive you and to continue the process of sanctification in your life. Accept His forgiveness and draw near to Him again in confident faith.

- The displacement of God from His rightful position in our lives is often gradual and can happen without our realizing it. Take some time to examine your life to see what is most important to you, what your priorities are, and how you are spending your time. God deserves our primary love, respect, and devotion. Write down anything you think you are putting ahead of God in your life, such as money, a relationship, or your career. Offer it to God and begin to renew your love and commitment to Him this week by spending extra time worshipping Him and acknowledging His fatherhood and sovereignty in your life.

- If you find yourself beginning to doubt after you have prayed, consciously replace those doubts with what the Word of God says about your situation.

"Let us throw off everything that hinders and the sin that so easily entangles."
—Hebrews 12:1

Part IV
The Power of Prayer

Chapter Ten
The Power of the Word

God wants to use His power in the world. However, for Him to do so, we must understand how to appropriate His Word.

CHAPTER THEME

O nce we understand our role as God's mediators for the world and have dealt with areas in our lives that block our prayers, we need to make sure we truly understand the power behind prayer: God's Word, the name of Jesus, and the Holy Spirit. This chapter focuses on the power of the Word.

Question for Reflection

1. Do you think of the Word of God as being alive and active on your behalf? Why or why not?

Exploring God's Principles and Purposes

2. What principle has been interwoven throughout this book and is a basis for this chapter? (p. 185)

3. Complete the following: True prayer is calling forth what God has already _____ and _____—the _____ of His plans for the earth. (p. 186)

4. God's purpose is to be both the _____ and _____ of our prayers. (p. 186)

5. What kind of prayers are powerless to effect change? (p. 186)

6. God has already given us His Word. It is our job to understand how to handle it _____ and _____. (pp. 186–87)

7. There are several aspects to the Word of God that we need to understand in order to apply it to our prayers effectively. What is the first aspect? (p. 187)

8. God's _____ becomes a part of our prayers when we speak His Word in faith. (p. 187)

9. God's Word is the _____ of His power. (p. 187)

10. What is the second aspect of the Word of God in relation to prayer? (p. 187)

11. What does Dr. Munroe describe as a "cardinal principle of answered prayer"? (pp. 187–88)

12. Belief is _____ in _____. (p. 188)

13. Name the third aspect of the Word of God in relation to prayer. (p. 188)

14. Give some biblical examples of the power of the Word. (pp. 189–90)

15. If we want the Word to work powerfully in our lives, what should we do? (p. 190)

16. What are two conditions of answered prayer found in John 15:7? (p. 191)

17. What does it mean to abide in Jesus? (p. 191)

18. What does it mean to have Jesus' words abiding or living in us? (p. 191)

19. If God's Word is within us, what kind of prayers will we pray? (p. 191)

20. Name the fourth aspect of the Word of God in relation to prayer. (p. 192)

21. When the Word of God is lived and practiced in our lives, it becomes _____ to us. (p. 192)

22. Faith in God and His Word— [choose one] (p. 192)

    (a) needs to be developed.

    (b) needs to be fed if we are to be spiritually sustained.

    (c) needs to be acted upon.

    (d) all of the above.

23. What you know from God's Word is more important than what you _____. (p. 193)

24. Faith enables us to receive God's _____. (pp. 194–95)

25. Belief will _____ _____ that hard work cannot unlock. (p. 195)

26. Who does God hear when we pray His Word? (p. 196)

27. What does 1 John 5:15 tell us happens when God hears our prayers? (p. 196)

28. What did Jesus say about the words He spoke? (p. 196)

29. Name the fifth aspect of the Word of God in relation to prayer. (p. 197)

30. The men and women of the Bible— [choose one] (p. 197)

    (a) had an advantage over us.

    (b) were super-saints.

    (c) were people just like us.

    (d) were God's favorites.

31. What are the implications for prayer that *"God does not show favoritism"* (Acts 10:34)? (p. 197)

32. What advantages do believers today have over God's people in the Old Testament? (p. 197)

33. What can the example of believers in the Bible do for us? (p. 198)

34. Name the sixth aspect of the Word of God in relation to prayer. (p. 199)

35. What happens when we wholeheartedly embrace God's Word? (p. 199)

36. What else do we need to do to have continual fellowship with God, according to Romans 12:1? (p. 199)

37. According to Romans 12:2, how can we know what God's will is so we can pray effectively? (p. 199)

Conclusion

The Word of God is a tremendous gift to us. It gives us the power to know and do the will of God, the power to pray with certainty and boldness, and the power to know that God hears and answers us when we pray according to His will.

Applying God's Principles to Your Life

Thinking It Over

- A cardinal principle of answered prayer is belief in the trustworthiness of the One to whom you're praying. Do you believe that God is honorable and that He will keep His Word? Why or why not?

- When you read in the Bible about God answering the prayers of His people, do you allow these accounts to build your faith for your own circumstances, or do you think of them merely as some interesting stories? How will you look at these accounts in the future, based on what you have learned in this chapter?

- Do you tend to live by faith in God and His Word or by what you see—circumstances, problems, the world around you? In what ways has reading this chapter changed your perspective on this?

Praying about It

- The Word will work in your life as you believe it; the power of your prayers depends on your faith in what God has said. Romans 14:23 says, *"Everything that does not come from faith is sin."* Ask God to bring to mind a situation about which you are worrying, despairing, or depending on your own ability. Ask Him to forgive you for not trusting Him and to strengthen you in your faith as you seek and rely on Him for this circumstance. Remember these two Scriptures: *"We know and rely on the love God has for us"* (1 John 4:16). *"The LORD delights in those who fear him, who put their hope in his unfailing love"* (Ps. 147:11).

- Meditate on verses that speak to the various needs we have in life so you may build your faith in God and His Word before (or as) problems arise. Here are some examples: *wisdom*—James 1:5; *salvation*—John 3:16; *healing*—1 Peter 2:24; *finances*—Philippians 4:19; *provision*—Matthew 7:11. Use these and other Scriptures as the basis for your prayers.

Acting on God's Truth

- We know the Word is truly inside us when it directs our thoughts and actions. What is the first thing that comes out of your mouth when you are under pressure? Is it an affirmation of faith, or is it fear, confusion, frustration, doubt, or anger? The next time you face a difficult situation, ask the Holy Spirit to direct you to Scriptures that address what you are going through. Meditate on these Scriptures and allow them to fill your mind and heart and strengthen your faith.

- Focus this week on abiding in Christ and having His words abide in you (John 15:7), so that the Word can be inside you to work powerfully in your life. Spend time worshipping and fellowshipping with God, reading and mediating on His Word, praying and fasting. Make these practices an ongoing part of your life.

- Examine the lives of three people in the Bible who offered effectual prayers to God. (See page 198 for examples.) What were their prayers like? What were their lives like? What had God promised them? What did God show or do for them in answering their prayers? Write down your findings and refer to them for encouragement and inspiration as you face challenging situations.

The Word prepares the pray-er for prayer.

Chapter Eleven
The Power of Jesus' Name

We must be able to legally use the authority behind the power of Jesus' name in order to obtain results in prayer.

CHAPTER THEME

One of the most important elements of effective prayer is using the name of Jesus, as He has told us to do: *"I tell you the truth, my Father will give you whatever you ask in my name. Until now you have not asked for anything in my name. Ask and you will receive, and your joy will be complete"* (John 16:23–24). In conjunction with praying according to the Word, praying in the name of Jesus gives our prayers tremendous power.

Question for Reflection

1. When you pray, do you pray "in Jesus' name"? What is the significance of praying in this way? Have you seen results from the prayers you've prayed in the name of Jesus? Why or why not?

Exploring God's Principles and Purposes

2. Circle One: True or False

    The phrase "in Jesus' name," in itself, makes our prayers effective with God. (p. 203)

    Explain your answer: (pp. 203–4)

3. What two things do we learn from the account of the sons of Sceva regarding how to "legally" use the authority behind the power of Jesus' name? (p. 204)

4. On what basis do we have authority in prayer in Jesus' name? (p. 205)

5. Name a Scripture passage in which Jesus gave us the legal right to use His name when making our requests to God. (p. 206)

6. Complete the following: Christ restored us to our relationship and rights with both God and the earth. Therefore, His name is our legal authority—whether we are dealing with *"heaven"* (with _____), *"earth"* (with _____), or *"under the earth"* (with _____). (p. 206)

7. In the Scriptures, what did the name of someone (or something) usually symbolize? (pp. 206–7)

8. God's name does not just represent who He is, but also, _____. (p. 208)

9. What is the significance of God's saying that His name is *"I Am"* (Exod. 3:14)? (pp. 208–9)

10. What is the significance of God's calling Himself *"the God of Abraham, the God of Isaac and the God of Jacob"* (Exod. 3:15)? (p. 209)

11. The names of the second person of the Trinity refer to all that He is, both as the _____ _____ _____ and as the _____ _____ _____—all of His nature, power, and glory. (p. 209)

12. The primary name of Christ in His divinity as the Son of God is _____ _____ while the primary name of Christ in His humanity as the Son of Man is _____. (p. 210)

13. Name a Scripture verse that connects Jesus with the I Am. (p. 210)

14. If we want God to meet our needs when we pray "in the name of Jesus," how must we pray? (p. 210)

15. Whatever our needs may be, God is telling us not to dwell on the _____, but on His _____ that addresses it. (p. 212)

16. For what reason did Dr. Munroe say we often lose out on many things in life? (p. 213)

17. How is praying in the name of Jesus like giving Him "power of attorney"? (p. 213)

18. When the Father answers our requests, whom does He work through? (p. 213)

19. From what position is Jesus working on our behalf in representing our interests to God? (pp. 213–14)

20. What Scripture assures us that Christ is interceding for us? (p. 214)

21. According to John 14:12–13, why did Jesus say He would answer the requests we pray in His name in faith? (p. 214)

22. How does the Holy Spirit assist in exercising power of attorney on our behalf? (p. 214)

23. If the Holy Spirit counsels us *not* to pray for something, we should— [choose one] (p. 215)

    (a) go ahead and ask anyway.

    (b) try to make it happen in our own strength.

    (c) not ask for what we were going to ask.

    (d) try to change God's mind.

    Explain your answer: (p. 215)

24. What is an important reason we don't have to worry about our "cases" being heard when the Son is representing us? (p. 215)

25. Jesus' name is the key to _____. (p. 215)

26. Circle one: True or False (p. 216)

    No one but Jesus can be our legal channel to the Father.

27. What Scripture tells us that Jesus is the only One who can speak for us to the Father? (p. 216)

28. What is the significance in terms of prayer and fulfilling God's purposes that Jesus' name is the *"name that is above every name"* and that *"at the name of Jesus every knee should bow, in heaven and on earth and under the earth"* (Phil. 2:9–10)? (pp. 216–17)

Conclusion

There is no other name by which we should make our requests to God the Father but the name of Jesus. Whatever we need, we may call on Jesus to fulfill that need based on who He is. We must use what He has provided for us when we ask the Father to manifest His power in our lives and in the lives of others: the ability to make our requests based on God's nature and attributes, and the authority to pray in Jesus' name.

Applying God's Principles to Your Life

Thinking It Over

• Have you ever prayed in the name of Jesus without thinking about what that name really means? How will you pray in the name of Jesus in the future based on what you have learned in this chapter?

- Do you know Jesus only as Savior and not also in relation to His other attributes? What specific attributes of Jesus meet your particular needs today?

- How does knowing that Jesus has "power of attorney" with God regarding your circumstances change the way you view them?

Praying about It

- Ask God to forgive you through Christ if you have taken the name of Jesus lightly or misused His name in prayer. Then, purpose in your heart always to honor Jesus' name in both your life and your prayers.

- When you pray, consciously give over your questions, concerns, and problems to Jesus as you pray about them in His name, reminding yourself that He has power of attorney with God and is interceding on your behalf.

- Romans 8:27 tells us that *"the Spirit intercedes for the saints in accordance with God's will,"* Ephesians 6:18 instructs us to *"pray in the Spirit on all occasions with all kinds of prayers and requests,"* and Jude 20 says, *"Build yourselves up in your most holy faith and pray in the Holy Spirit."* Are you making your requests to God guided by the Holy Spirit, or are you praying to Him in your own strength and wisdom? Begin today to ask God's Spirit to help you pray. Then, *"pray in the Spirit on all occasions"* as you pray in Jesus' name.

- The Scripture says, *"Everyone who calls on the name of the Lord will be saved"* (Acts 2:21). If you want someone among your family and friends to be saved, then pray on his or her behalf in the name of the *Savior.*

Acting on God's Truth

- The attributes of Jesus reveal His glory and correspond to His people's needs. Jesus' attributes are as numerous as your needs—and beyond! Meditate on the various names of Jesus, including these that follow, so that you will be able to pray for your needs and others' needs according to who Jesus is.

Jesus is—

Wonderful Counselor (Isa. 9:6)

Mighty God (Isa. 9:6)

Prince of Peace (Isa. 9:6)

Lamb of God (John 1:29)

The Bread of Life (John 6:35)

The Water of Life (John 7:37)

The Way, the Truth, and the Life (John 14:6)

The True Vine (John 15:1)

Alpha and Omega, the First and the Last (Rev. 22:13)

- Do you tend to dwell on your problems rather than on the attributes of God that can address them? If you are going through a difficult time now, or the next time you find yourself facing a trying situation, think and pray about the circumstance based on the attribute of God that can meet it.

- Jesus is the Resurrection and the Life. Is there anything in your life that you may have "declared dead" prematurely? Ask God to help you pray about any such situations, aided by the Holy Spirit, so that He can breathe new life into the circumstance according to His will.

"Until now you have not asked for anything in my name.
Ask and you will receive, and your joy will be complete."
—John 16:24

Chapter Twelve
Understanding Fasting

A fast is a conscious, intentional decision to abstain for a time from the pleasure of eating in order to gain vital spiritual benefits.

CHAPTER THEME

Fasting is one of the pillars of the Christian faith. It is mentioned in Scripture one-third as much as prayer. Yet, while fasting used to be seen as valuable and significant in the Christian church, it has now become a lost art. The majority of us put fasting in the background of our spiritual experience, while many consider the regular practice of fasting to be almost fanatical. So little is taught and practiced in the church today in regard to fasting that it is not understood by most believers, especially new Christians. They don't hear about or see many older believers fasting, so they conclude that it is something that has only historic significance. In addition, while many believers admire the spiritual effectiveness of Moses, Daniel, Paul, Peter, and other historical people of faith, they often don't realize that prayer and fasting was what brought about the manifestation of such spiritual power in their lives. This chapter provides an overview of what fasting is, why God says we are to fast, and how fasting relates to prayer.

Questions for Reflection

1. Do you practice fasting on a regular basis, or have you fasted in the past? Why or why not? What was your motivation for fasting or not fasting?

2. Do you tend to fast for specific purposes or problems? If so, what are they? Why do you think it is important to fast for them?

Exploring God's Principles and Purposes

3. Circle one: True or False

   Fasting should be a natural part of the lives of believers in the same way that they practice the habits of reading the Bible and prayer. (p. 222)

4. Complete the following: Prayer and fasting are _____ _____ of a _____ ministry. (p. 222)

5. How do we know that fasting is an expectation God has for His people rather than an option? (p. 222)

6. Circle one: True or False

   We should wait for a special prompting from God before we fast. (p. 222)

   Explain your answer: (p. 222)

7. What is the definition of a fast? (p. 223)

8. There are four key purposes of fasting. What is the first one? (p. 223)

9. Fasting means abstaining from other things that you find pleasure in for the purpose of giving your _____ _____ to God in prayer. (p. 223)

10. What is the second purpose of fasting? (p. 223)

11. How do we show God that we are putting Him first? (p. 223)

12. How is fasting a point of intimacy with God? (p. 223)

13. The third purpose of fasting is for _____ _____. (p. 224)

14. List some biblical examples in which fasting contributed to an environment in which God worked on behalf of His people. (p. 224)

15. Name the fourth purpose of fasting. (p. 224)

16. What is the *main* purpose of fasting? (p. 224)

17. What is one way in which fasting goes beyond just praying? (p. 224)

18. We _____ ourselves of food in order to _____ ourselves with God. (p. 225)

19. Fasting enables us to— [choose one] (p. 225)

    (a) increase our spiritual capacity.

    (b) exert discipline over our physical appetites.

    (c) bring the body under subjection to what the spirit desires.

    (d) all of the above

20. Circle one: True or False

    Fasting does not change God; it changes us, and it transforms our prayers. (p. 226)

21. What is the first of three main results we receive through fasting? (p. 226)

22. Name the second main result of fasting. (p. 226)

23. Why is prayer, by itself, sometimes not enough to accomplish God's purposes? (pp. 226–27)

24. Why is it important for us to fast on a regular basis—and especially when we feel spiritually dry and lifeless? (pp. 227–28)

25. Difficult problems and people who need special ministry sometimes come our way during or after a fast. Why is this the case? (p. 228)

26. What is the third main result of fasting? (p. 228)

27. Why do you think God's answer for the Israelites was to *"declare a holy fast"* (Joel 1:14) when nothing was going right for them, and they had lost their joy? (pp. 228–29)

28. How do we know that God will answer when we fast and repent before Him during difficult circumstances? (pp. 229–30)

29. We need to be careful not to hinder the effectiveness of our fasts by having the wrong spirit when we are fasting. List some right and wrong ways to fast based on what God told the Israelites in Isaiah 58. (pp. 231–33)

30. What are the outcomes of a true fast? (pp. 232–33)

Conclusion

Are you tired of praying, and seeing no results? When you fast, you're setting yourself up for answered prayer. God has promised that if you fast in the right way, He will hear and answer. *"Then you will call, and the LORD will answer; you will cry for help, and he will say: Here am I"* (Isa. 58:9).

Why will God answer your prayers? When you fast, you are open to Him. Your spiritual capacity to hear and receive is increased. You are empty of your own interests, and you are ready for Him to fill you.

Applying God's Principles to Your Life

Thinking It Over

- Do your prayers—and even your fasting—tend to focus on yourself or on others? How could a true fast enable you to be more aware of the needs of others and intercede for them?

- Is there a situation in your life, or a person for whom you are praying, that has not yet responded to prayer? What have you learned in this chapter about the breakthroughs fasting can bring about in such circumstances?

- Are you experiencing a spiritually dry period in your life in which you have little desire to worship and serve God? How can fasting renew you spiritually?

- When you fast, are you setting aside time to consecrate yourself to God, or are you allowing yourself to become distracted with other concerns and activities? How does God respond when we "do as we please" when we fast? How can you be more consecrated to God during your fasts?

Praying about It

- Begin to add fasting to your prayer life. To make fasting a true spiritual habit, you may want to start with one meal or one day a week and gradually increase the time you fast. Be sure to set aside what would have been the meal time, as well as other times of the day, to consecrate yourself to God and seek Him.

- After reviewing the "right" and "wrong" ways to fast, ask yourself if you have been fasting in a way that is pleasing to God. If not, ask Him to forgive you for not entering into a true fast, and to enable you to seek Him with your whole heart the next time you fast.

- As you make fasting a spiritual habit, write down how fasting changes both you and your prayer life.

- Write down how God increases your spiritual capacity for hearing Him, fellowshipping with Him, and receiving power in ministry through fasting.

Acting on God's Truth

- What difficult circumstance are you facing, or what people have you been praying for who have been resistant to the Gospel? Are you willing to "pay the price" to receive God's answer concerning the situation? Set aside a time to consecrate yourself in prayer and fasting to let God know you are serious about this concern and are totally dependent on Him for help. Thank Him in advance for His answer.

- Compare Isaiah 58:6–9 with 1 John 3:14–19 and Matthew 25:31–40. In what ways do the New Testament passages reinforce what God said in Isaiah is important to Him during a fast? Write the similarities below:

• Considering the kind of fast that pleases God, what is one way you can help meet someone's spiritual or physical needs this week? What can you do to bring justice and comfort to others on a more regular basis?

"Declare a holy fast."
—Joel 1:14

Answer Key

Chapter One
Does Prayer Really Work?

1. Answers will vary.
2. Answers will vary.
3. Answers will vary.
4. Answers will vary.
5. unanswered prayer
6. religious exercise; results
7. We can measure how much the average Christian believes in the effectiveness of prayer by the small number of people who attend prayer meetings in our churches.
8. teaching; interest; understanding
9. They simply don't know how or why to pray, or they know some of the principles of prayer but are not fulfilling their full potential as intercessors because they don't understand key aspects of prayer.
10. (1) We feel abandoned and isolated from God, imagining that He doesn't care about our problems. (2) We question God's character and integrity (and His Word). (3) We feel as if our lives are very unsettled and unstable. (For this reason, we rely on ourselves and others rather than on God.) (4) We come to premature conclusions about ourselves and our prayers. (Because of these assumptions, we fail to learn God's principles and truths about prayer.) (5) We doubt our calling as God's intercessors.
11. Some effects of confusion over prayer are powerlessness, lack of direction, little victory over sin, poor spiritual progress, a weak witness, unfruitful ministry, and poverty.

12. (c) communion and communication with God that touches His heart

13. Prayer has the power to transform lives, change circumstances, give peace and perseverance in the midst of trial, alter the course of nations, and win the world for Christ.

14. inheritance

15. True

16. False

17. Jesus said, *"Therefore I tell you, whatever you ask for in prayer, believe that you have received it, and it will be yours"* (Mark 11:24).

18. God's will and Word work in our lives when they are understood and put into practice.

19. True prayer builds intimacy with God; brings honor to His nature and character; causes respect for His integrity; enables belief in His Word; causes trust in His love; affirms His purposes and will; appropriates His promises.

20. At times, God will withhold answers to prayer so we will seek Him and the principles of prayer that are essential for praying according to His will and for appropriating His promises and power.

21. ineffective

22. or else God would not ask us to pray

23. Jesus said, *"Father, I thank you that you have heard me. I knew that you always hear me"* (John 11:41–42).

Chapter Two
The Genesis of Prayer

1. Answers will vary.

2. purpose; arbitrary

3. Answers may vary, but should include the following ideas: First, humanity was created not only to reflect God's nature, but also to have fellowship with Him through a relationship of love. Second, mankind was created to share God's authority; humanity was created to carry out God's purposes in the earth and to have dominion over it. The account of the creation of mankind shows us that God never desired or intended to rule the earth by Himself. The *relationship of love*

that God established with mankind is not separate from the *purpose* God has for mankind. Rather, the relationship is foundational to the purpose, and both are essential keys to the reason for prayer: fellowship and dominion.

4. God wants us to approach Him as a child would a loving father.

5. Human beings were meant to carry out God's purposes for the earth using their own wills and initiative. They were to reflect the God who plans in advance and carries out His plans through creative acts.

6. Humanity is to carry out dominion in the earthly or physical realm and in the spiritual realm.

7. We are to take the character of the Garden—God's presence, light, and truth—and spread it throughout the world. Isaiah 11:9 says, *"The earth will be full of the knowledge of the LORD as the waters cover the sea."*

8. connected

9. for; with

10. offspring; servants; sons; daughters

11. It means we are to cooperate, help, and work together with Him.

12. Some people think prayer originated because we were separated from God by our sin through the fall of mankind, and we needed a means by which to reconnect with Him.

13. Reconnecting to God after the fall of mankind is one use for prayer, but it is not the heart of prayer because prayer began with the *creation* of mankind, before the Fall.

14. Prayer is an expression of mankind's unity and relationship of love with God, and an expression of mankind's affirmation of and participation in God's purposes for the earth.

15. Union with God means unity and singleness of purpose, thought, desire, will, reason, motive, objective, and feelings.

16. affects; affected by

17. The essence of the very first prayer was the fellowship between God and Adam, and Adam's agreement with God's purposes.

18. Because of the fall of mankind and our own sin nature, we often need to prepare our hearts in prayer in order to enter God's presence (through worship, confession, and so

forth). Yet prayer doesn't only bring us into God's presence; it is communion with Him in a unity of love and purpose while we are in His presence. This is the prayer life that Adam had before the Fall.

19. Prayer is essential for the fulfillment of God's purposes in the earth because of the way God arranged dominion and authority. God made men and women and gave them dominion over all the works of His hands. Mankind was given full authority in the earth realm, and God will not supercede that authority. When God said, *"Let them rule...over all the earth"* (Gen. 1:26), He was ordering the dominion of the world in such a way as to make the rule of humans essential for the accomplishment of His purposes. He causes things to happen on earth when men and women are in agreement with His will. In this way, He placed His will for the earth on the cooperation of the will of man.

20. mandatory; optional

21. Prayer is earthly license for heavenly interference.

22. backbone; center; heart; source; strength

23. His will through your will

24. The key to effective prayer is understanding God's purpose for your life, His reason for your existence—as a human being in general and as an individual specifically.

25. It becomes the "raw material," the foundational matter, for your prayer life.

26. purposed; predestined

27. We often pray in the wrong way because we aren't asking for the right things. We are not to ask God to do anything outside of what we have been given to do based on our purpose. If we ask for things that are contrary to our purpose, we will be frustrated.

28. Jesus' assurance in prayer was based on His knowing and doing God's will.

29. God grants what we ask of Him.

30. We allow God's purposes for the world to be hindered. We need to ask God to intervene in human affairs because, if we don't, our world will be susceptible to the influences of Satan and sin.

31. True

32. We are failing to fulfill our role in God's purposes.

33. The image and likeness of God within man is marred, and the purposes of God for the world are obstructed—purposes of goodness, fruitfulness, creativity, truth, joy, and love.

34. Satan tempted the first man and woman to disobey God, and they chose to agree with his purposes rather than with God's. In doing so, mankind sinned and cut off communion with God. Humanity no longer agreed with God to fulfill His purposes for the earth—leaving the world at the mercy of a renegade authority that no longer had God's best interests in mind. In fact, man forfeited his authority to Satan, whom he had chosen to serve in place of God. That meant that the Fall introduced a new ruler on earth—one bent on its destruction rather than its growth in godliness and fruitfulness. This is why the Bible refers to Satan as *"the god of this world"* (2 Cor. 4:4 KJV).

35. Their effectiveness in prayer was also broken.

36. relationship

37. Our difficulties with prayer may be traced to the Fall and the resulting fallen nature of man, through which we were estranged from God.

38. Effective prayer has everything to do with being united with God in a relationship of love, having a heart and mind in union with God's will, gaining a discerning mind in regard to His purposes, and exercising faith in His Word. Since these things are contrary to the fallen nature, we need to be renewed in our minds concerning them.

Chapter Three
The Authority of Prayer

1. Answers will vary.
2. Answers will vary.
3. (e) all of the above
4. You can conclude that your concept of prayer has been influenced by the effects of the Fall.
5. God did not simply wrench control of the earth back from Satan because that action would have been inconsistent with

the integrity of His character and purposes. In addition, the devil could have accused Him of doing what he had done— usurping the authority that was given to man in creation. God has *all* power and authority. Yet He has given mankind authority over the earth, as well as a free will, and He will not rescind or usurp those gifts—even though man sinned, rejected Him, and deserved to be separated from Him forever. God respected the authority He had given mankind even when it lay dormant within man's fallen nature, for *"God's gifts and his call are irrevocable"* (Rom. 11:29).

6. First, man's sin would have to be dealt with. Second, man would also have to *want* to return to God and work together with Him out of his own free will.

7. purposes; pray; authority

8. We may approach God with freedom and confidence when we do so through faith in Christ.

9. Jesus had to come as a Representative of the legal authority of the earth—man. He had to come as a *human being,* as the Second Adam, as the beginning of a new family of mankind who would be devoted to God—*"the firstborn among many brothers"* (Rom. 8:29).

10. Only a perfectly righteous man who desired to do God's will could redeem humanity and restore its relationship with God. Therefore, Jesus had to be without sin, and He had to *choose* to do the will of God—which He did. The Bible says, *"God made him who had no sin to be sin for us, so that in him we might become the righteousness of God"* (2 Cor. 5:21).

11. Christ is the image of God.

12. humanity; divinity

13. Christ has a deep relationship of love with God.

14. *I and the Father are one*

15. He lives to do God's will

16. It reminds us of the connection between love for God and oneness with His purposes.

17. Christ reigns with authority.

18. True. Jesus has the right and the power to reign on the earth and to ask God to intervene in the world since He was the perfect Man and the perfect Sacrifice. His prayers for mankind are powerful and effective. He has also given

believers His Spirit so that we can agree with God's purposes even when we are uncertain about how to pray. In addition, as lawful King of the earth, Jesus ultimately has the right to silence anyone who opposes God.

19. Jesus reclaimed mankind's earthly authority.

20. First, Jesus came as a man and was therefore qualified as a Representative of earthly authority. Second, Jesus was perfectly obedient and sinless. He was therefore qualified to be the Son of God and to restore man's relationship with the Father by overcoming sin and death through His sacrifice on the cross. Third, Jesus rose victoriously and was therefore qualified to defeat sin and Satan, regain authority over the earth, and be the earth's rightful King.

21. transferred authority to those who believe

22. The redeemed person is now in a position to enter fully into a relationship of love with God and to agree that "His kingdom come, His will be done on earth as it is in heaven." (See Matthew 6:10.)

23. Through mankind, God desires to reveal His character, nature, principles, precepts, and righteousness to the visible world.

24. False. At the culmination of the age, when God resurrects the bodies of believers and reunites them with their spirits, and when He creates the new heavens and earth, it will be for the purpose of enabling man to truly fulfill his calling and vocation. The Scripture says we will reign with Jesus *"for ever and ever"* (Rev. 22:5). To reign means to have dominion, to administrate. Therefore, as we live and work in this fallen world today and, in the future, when we will live and reign with Jesus, the commission from God is the same: *"Let them rule...over all the earth"* (Gen. 1:26).

25. We do not recognize—or accept—our calling and authority as *"ministers of a new covenant"* (2 Cor. 3:6), which we have received in Christ. Our fear of being proud or presumptuous about what we have been given in Christ, along with our lack of acceptance of our worth in Him, have kept us in bondage and robbed us of the reality of His finished work on our behalf—which enables us to fulfill God's purposes in the world.

26. Satan has no authority over us.
27. live; belong
28. authority; name
29. Sin has no authority over us.
30. Grace now reigns instead of sin.
31. we have authority through Jesus' name
32. access; name
33. First, we can enjoy a restored relationship with God. Second, we can now agree with the Father and His purposes, and ask Him to fulfill His Word as He meets our needs and the needs of others.
34. We have authority through the Word.
35. False. When we pray in Jesus' name, we must also pray according to God's will, which we find in His Word. (See John 15:7.)
36. The backbone of prayer is composed of our agreement with God's Word, our oneness with Christ, who is the Living Word, and our unity with God's purposes and will.
37. promises
38. model
39. Jesus did not have an advantage over us in regard to prayer and living for God. What He accomplished on earth, He accomplished in His humanity (as the Son of Man), not in His divinity. Otherwise, He could not have been man's Representative and Substitute.
40. Jesus kept a close relationship with the Father through prayer; He did what God directed Him to do and what He saw God actively working to accomplish in the world; He relied on the grace and Spirit of God. We can do the same.
41. John 14:10–14
42. As He did for Jesus, God will reveal to us what He is doing in the world and how our purposes are related to His overall purpose.
43. Christ provides us with a relationship of love with God the Father, the certainty of our redemption in Christ, an understanding of our calling and authority in Christ, and a clear idea of God's purpose for our lives.
44. It is not only our calling in creation, but also our redemption in Christ, that gives us the right to pray to God.

Chapter Four
How to Enter God's Presence

1. Answers will vary.
2. Answers will vary.
3. (b) they often do not have a genuine reverence for God.
4. Answers will vary.
5. We misunderstand the nature of grace in relation to the law, believing that grace gives us a license to sin. We treat Christ's sacrifice for our sins lightly so that, instead of loving and obeying Him, we "use" Him to fix the messes we create for ourselves.
6. Grace supersedes law in the sense that only the grace we receive in Christ enables us to *fulfill* God's law.
7. An apathetic attitude toward God may cause Him not to answer our prayers.
8. We should obey God not because we want things from Him but because we love Him.
9. Holiness is critical to prayer because *"without holiness no one will see the Lord"* (Heb. 12:14).
10. "Seeing" God refers to having an intimate relationship of love with Him and entering into His presence so we can know His heart and mind.
11. The word *holy* means to "sanctify, or set apart," or "to be set."
12. To be pure or holy in heart means that your mind is set on God and His ways.
13. We are to be holy because God is holy, and we were created to reflect His nature and ways and to be set apart for His purposes. (See Leviticus 11:44; 20:26.)
14. We are to "fix" ourselves on God and not be influenced by people who are not set on Him and who do not believe His Word.
15. Holiness is being convinced that what God says and what God does are the same. If your mind is set in regard to your prayers—that is, if you are convinced that God will do what He has promised you, if you are pure both in what you believe and in what you do—then you will see God's works manifested.

16. There is an inconsistency between what he says and what he actually believes and does.

17. integrity; say; do; telling; living

18. Our prayers will not be answered because we show that we doubt God's integrity.

19. Since we know that God is holy, we can believe He will fulfill what He has promised. This is because if God were not true to His Word, He would be acting in an unholy way. We can believe we will receive what we ask of Him according to His Word.

20. God has always purposed that all people be His "priests" in the world. Humanity is to be His representative and intermediary for the earth.

21. God raised up a Priest who would be faithful—Jesus, the second person of the Trinity, the Son of God, our High Priest. He served God perfectly. He knew how to enter God's presence and how to represent man to God and God to man. In doing so, He created a new nation of people who would be God's priests to the world. This nation is called the church.

22. *"You also, like living stones, are being built into a spiritual house to be a holy priesthood, offering spiritual sacrifices acceptable to God through Jesus Christ....But you are a chosen people, a royal priesthood, a holy nation, a people belonging to God, that you may declare the praises of him who called you out of darkness into his wonderful light"* (1 Pet. 2:5, 9).

23. Answers may vary, but should include the following ideas: Without holiness, we cannot be representatives or intermediaries of God because to do so requires having an intimate relationship of love with God, entering His presence in order to know His heart and mind, being set apart for His purposes, and believing He will do what He has promised.

24. Holy Spirit

25. The first step is to appropriate God's grace.

26. Our sins must be dealt with before we enter God's presence.

27. We need to clean out the secret closets of sin and disobedience within us. We need to understand and accept Christ's sacrifice for our sins and repent from wrongdoing. When we

do so, Christ covers us with His blood, and we are cleansed. We also need to be daily cleansed from our sins so we can live before God in holiness—the holiness Christ died to provide for us. First John 1:9 says, *"If we confess our sins, he is faithful and just and will forgive us our sins and purify us from all unrighteousness."*

28. *"But your iniquities have separated you from your God; your sins have hidden his face from you, so that he will not hear"* (Isa. 59:2).

29. When our sins are forgiven and we are right with God, we can genuinely fellowship with Him and with other believers—which brings the power of agreement in prayer.

30. The second step is to put on righteousness.

31. *"Put on the new self, created to be like God in true righteousness and holiness"* (Eph. 4:24).

32. We are able to come before God through Jesus' righteousness. We can enter God's presence only by appropriating the righteousness of Christ through faith: *"God made him who had no sin to be sin for us, so that in him we might become the righteousness of God"* (2 Cor. 5:21). In order to daily live in Christ's righteousness, we must "keep in step" with the Spirit. (See Galatians 5:22–25.)

33. put on truth and honesty

34. inner

35. The *"inner parts"* are the parts we don't like to talk about, the secret life only we know about.

36. We can be pure before God in our inner parts by turning from our sinful ways, receiving forgiveness through Christ, and walking in the Spirit. (See Romans 8:3–4.)

37. cleanse; Word

38. It means that we've *read* the Word, the Word is *in* us, and we are *obeying* the Word.

39. attitudes; actions

40. The fifth step is to worship and praise God.

41. Jesus said that true worshipers worship *"in spirit and in truth."*

42. Answers will vary, but should include the following ideas: Our worship of God is not a religious formula but the

communion of our spirits with God's Spirit. To be able to commune with God, who is holy and pure, we must have the righteousness of Christ and be seeking to obey God's Word. We also must seek God with the right motivation, which is love for Him and His ways.

43. The sixth step is to separate yourself.

44. We need to separate ourselves from our normal environment and activities as well as from distractions.

45. It is a place *in God.* We can enter this place if our hearts, attitudes, and motives are right—if our lives are right before Him.

46. We can fast.

47. When we fast, we eliminate distractions. We remove ourselves from many things that have been clogging up our lives and disturbing our spirits. We feel freer, less encumbered by the world. We have more time for God.

48. believe

49. To believe is to have faith in God's power to do what He has promised.

50. We can enter boldly into God's presence when we believe in the effectiveness of Christ's sacrifice on our behalf, knowing that the blood of Jesus has cleansed us from our sin.

51. The eighth step is to give God the glory.

52. We are confessing that He is the One who accomplished our forgiveness, atonement, cleansing, and redemption. We are confessing that He has made us fit to be in His presence where His glory is, and that He is worthy of all honor and praise.

53. (d) give it back to God so that others who have needs can be blessed

54. The ninth step is to wash in the Word.

55. The first use of the Word is for cleansing. The second is for appropriating God's promises.

56. We wash in the Word by asking God to fulfill His purposes based on His will and promises.

57. The tenth step is to remain in the anointing.

58. We can remain in His anointing by maintaining a right relationship with God, following His instructions and ways, so we may continually dwell in His presence.

59. We can remain in God's presence continually because of Christ's atonement for our sins. He was anointed and ordained as High Priest by God, and His atonement is fulfilled and sustained for all time. The atonement that He made is eternal; therefore it remains an everlasting ordinance. We can be continually cleansed from our sin and clean before the Lord as we appropriate Christ's sacrifice on our behalf.

Chapter Five
Cultivating the God Kind of Faith

1. Answers will vary.
2. Answers will vary.
3. True. Faith of some kind is working in the lives of everyone—believers in God and nonbelievers alike—whether we are aware of it or not.
4. The Word of God says, *"The just shall live by faith"* (Rom. 1:17 NKJV; Gal. 3:11 NKJV), and *"Without faith it is impossible to please God"* (Heb. 11:6).
5. In general terms, having faith means believing and having confidence in the words that you hear. It is believing in something that is not seen as though it is already a reality—and then speaking it and expecting it until it manifests itself.
6. God operates through words of faith.
7. God created by believing in the reality of what He would create before He saw its manifestation. He not only spoke words to create things, but He also uses words to keep the universe running. Hebrews 1:3 says that He sustains *"all things by his powerful word."* The principle for us is this: When we ask for something in prayer based on what God has promised, we have to start speaking about it as if it already exists. Moreover, we have to keep on speaking it in order to see its manifestation and to keep it from being "stolen" by the enemy.
8. heart; believe
9. God has given us the same ability He possesses—creative expression through our words. Just as God created His world with His words, so we create our worlds with our words.
10. expectation; action

11. God sometimes doesn't answer our prayers because He understands how powerful the principle of faith is and knows that what we're asking for wouldn't be good for us. He doesn't want us to have what is not right for us. He wants us to pray in a way that reflects the faith that He gives because such prayer is based on His good purposes for us.

12. "Have the God kind of faith."

13. False. Faith doesn't only initially come by hearing. It continues to come by continual hearing. Faith comes from the word that is near you.

14. listen; hear

15. The God kind of faith comes from "hearing" God's Word—listening to it, reading it, and believing it.

16. A constant diet of the Word of God will nourish your heart so that, when you experience troubles, the Word is what will come out of your mouth, and you will "create" what the Word says in the midst of the situation.

17. positively; negatively

18. You will likely get what you say. What you keep saying the most is what you will receive.

19. Answers may vary, but should include the following ideas: When we ask for something in prayer according to God's Word and promise, we must keep saying it and believing it, we must persevere in holding on to God's truth, until we see the reality manifested. When we do this, God will answer, and we won't be ashamed by not receiving what we have asked for. (See Romans 10:10–11.)

20. Spending time with people of faith will help nourish your own faith. It's difficult to start believing and then spend most of your time around people who aren't living in faith, because then you begin to pick up their attitudes, which can kill belief.

21. When we are connected to the Word of God, it will flow continuously into our lives. The result will be that we will bear "fruit" in its season. We might not see immediate answers to our prayers, but the season for their fulfillment is coming because the Word is flowing into our lives.

22. Faith is a ministry that God releases. He sends the word of faith, and He uses us to deliver it to others. When others

see what God has done in our lives through faith, they will ask us about the God of our faith.

23. The foremost source we should be listening to is the Word of God.

24. We've been trained to think that reality is only what we can see.

25. What God tells us in His Word is true reality, so we have to live according to faith in His Word to be living in reality.

26. Satan's goal is to feed us words contrary to God's words, thereby producing faith for destruction and death in our lives.

27. We need to be careful not to be influenced when people tell us what is contrary to the Word or why something can't be done, when God has said that it can. We must keep having faith in and affirming the truth of God's Word. We should keep believing and talking about the goodness of God and the impossibilities that God can bring to pass. The Bible says God fulfills His Word and *"calls things that are not as though they were"* (Rom. 4:17).

Chapter Six
Jesus' Model Prayer

1. Answers will vary.

2. The disciples saw that Jesus spent hours in prayer before performing miracles and healings that took a matter of seconds or minutes. They understood that the prayer that preceded the actions was what brought about the power for ministry.

3. True

4. (f) all of the above

5. Jesus said that everything He did stemmed from His intimacy with the Father in prayer; He did nothing from His own initiative. Jesus did only what He saw the Father doing, which the Father revealed to Him in prayer and communion with Him. Christ said, in essence, "I go to the Father first; I see what He's already done, and I do it."

6. Prayer is the medium through which man discovers what God has already done in the unseen so he can give heaven "permission" through his faith to manifest it on earth.

7. Jesus spent hours in prayer because He had a genuine relationship with the Father, and any relationship takes time to build and maintain.

8. God begins to use *us* to change circumstances.

9. (a) to our minds, through our spirits

10. God doesn't generally speak verbally because words are not intimate enough. He desires a close relationship with us—the communion of Spirit with spirit.

11. God has spoken to Dr. Munroe through thoughts, ideas, impressions, suggestions in his heart, sensing, and discernment.

12. relationship; responsibility; Corporate

13. False

14. True

15. model

16. The purpose of asking God to accomplish His will in the earth.

17. We are to begin prayer by thinking of others and their concerns as well as ourselves.

18. We are to go to God with the awareness and confession that He is the Source who can provide for whatever needs we or others may have.

19. First, we are confessing that we need external help—God's help—in our lives on earth, and that God is greater than we are. Second, we are confessing that, because the Father is not on the earth, we need an intermediary. We have to depend on Jesus and the Holy Spirit to be our intermediaries with God.

20. We are to worship the Father before making our requests, acknowledging and reverencing Him as the Holy One and as our all in all. We are to honor all the attributes of His holiness, such as His love, faithfulness, integrity, and grace. Then, after we pray, we are to continue to honor Him by the integrity of our lives and in all our interactions with others.

21. A true person of prayer is not interested in his own kingdom. His interest is in God's kingdom and what He wants accomplished. We should always ask for the fulfillment of God's "prayer list" before our own.

22. God will bless us in the course of accomplishing His work on earth and will meet all our needs.

23. Again, the plural used in this request is tied to the *"Our"* in *"Our Father."* We have already told God that we are coming to Him with the concerns of other people as well as ourselves. Therefore, when we ask for bread, we have to ask for bread not only for ourselves, but also for others.

24. It refers not only to food, but also to all aspects of what we need for daily health and sustenance.

25. Answers may vary, but should include the following ideas: Our prayers have to take into consideration those with whom we are in relationship. We can't harbor unforgiveness and bitterness against others and then expect God to forgive us and to hear our prayers. The Bible says that if we regard iniquity in our hearts, the Lord will not hear us (Ps. 66:18 KJV). This is because God is a God of love, forgiveness, and holiness, and we must reflect His nature and character. We have to follow His ways if we want to be in true relationship with Him.

26. relationships

27. The Bible says, *"The only thing that counts is faith expressing itself through love"* (Gal. 5:6). In other words, faith does not exist in a vacuum. It is part of the expression of the nature of God, who *"is love"* (1 John 4:8, 16). We must have both love and faith working in harmony for our prayers to be answered.

28. No, God never tempts us. (See James 1:13–15.) It means we need to be alert to the temptations and weaknesses that could harm our relationships with God and our testimony for Him, things that Satan wants to exploit to cause us to stumble. Then we need to pray that God will protect us from succumbing to those temptations and weaknesses.

29. We are to ask God for wisdom and strength to stop making bad decisions so we won't put ourselves into situations that will tempt us to sin and cause us to compromise our relationship with Him. We are also to *"put on the full armor of God so that* [we] *can take* [our] *stand against the devil's schemes"* (Eph. 6:11; see verses 12–18).

30. By worshipping God again, we're acknowledging to Him that He will answer our prayers, and we're thanking Him ahead of time, giving Him all the glory for how, why, and when He answers.

Chapter Seven
Twelve Action Steps to Prayer

1. Answers will vary.
2. The first step is to become silent. To be silent means to gather oneself, to be still—to focus your thoughts, attention, and concentration.
3. We are to go to a quiet and private place where we will not be disturbed and where we can eliminate distractions.
4. Prayer is the expression of man's dependency upon God for all things.
5. We will be unable to pray God's will with singleness of purpose.
6. heart; purpose
7. The second action step is to give adoration.
8. We are to worship God for who He is—King of all the earth, our Creator, our Savior, our all in all—expressing in our own words how precious He is to us.
9. make confession
10. Confession means agreeing with God about what He says *to* you and *about* you.
11. When we enter into God's presence through adoration, He starts shining His light on sins and wrong attitudes in our lives that we thought were hidden from Him. It is God who prompts what we are to confess. We can agree with God only when we can hear what He is saying to us, and adoration makes us open to hear Him.
12. False. God doesn't want us to feel condemned but instead to agree with Him that what we've been doing is wrong and then *stop doing it*. God will then forgive us and restore us to right standing with Him. (See 1 John 1:9.) We are also to put our trust in God to enable us to obey Him by walking by the Spirit. (See Galatians 5:16.)
13. acknowledge; holding; doing

14. If we don't acknowledge, confess, and turn away from our sin, it can destroy us. What we have been desiring in life may never happen, for we will be the ruination of our own pursuits.

15. condemn

16. The fourth action step is to give thanks.

17. If we have confessed before God, then our hearts are right, and we can offer righteous sacrifices of praise to Him. We can give thanks abundantly because our hearts are free. Since God has forgiven us of so much, we will always have something to be thankful for.

18. make supplication

19. When we offer supplication, it means we feel the heart of God. God shows us some of what He's feeling, and we become unified with His purposes and desires so that we wholeheartedly agree with Him in prayer to fulfill His will.

20. When we give thanks, we usually move into supplication because thanksgiving pleases God, and therefore He reveals to us what is in His heart.

21. The sixth action step is to specify petitions and requests.

22. intentional

23. evidence; relevant

24. We can specify our petitions by acknowledging God's name and Word in relation to them. One way we can do this is to write down what we are praying for, along with Scriptures about God's name or promises that apply to them.

25. The seventh action step is to secure the promises.

26. This step involves holding on to God's promises as we take His Word before Him, applying it to the particular requests we are making.

27. plead the case

28. False

29. Jesus wanted to illustrate the fact that having our prayers answered doesn't have anything to do with God "liking" us or not. God answers prayer when we qualify through faith in His promises and righteous living, and because of the fact that God is holy and keeps His Word.

30. God wants us to come to prayer with an attitude that says, "You're the only One who can help me." Often, we pray

for God's help, but we have a backup plan, just in case. God often does not answer until we have no other place to turn but to Him, so that we will know that He is our Provider and that we must depend completely on Him.

31. justice; promises; inheritance

32. The ninth step is to believe.

33. When we ask, we are to believe right then and there that we have already received what we have asked for.

34. When we truly believe that we *have received* what we asked for, it will be ours.

35. give thanks

36. The first thanksgiving expresses our appreciation for God's forgiveness and mercy. The second thanksgiving is the highest form of faith. We thank God for what we don't yet see because we believe it is already done.

37. manifestation; gratitude

38. The eleventh step is to live in expectation.

39. We are to anticipate the answers to our prayers by preparing the way for them. We are to make arrangements for our answers, according to the specific prayers we have prayed.

40. practice active belief

41. Luke 11:9: *"Ask and it will be given to you; seek and you will find; knock and the door will be opened to you."*

42. We are not to stop after we have prayed, but we are to get up and "look" for what we asked for. If we seek and knock, it will come to pass. Practicing active belief shows that we are living in expectation.

Chapter Eight
Hurdles to Answered Prayer

1. Answers will vary.

2. Answers will vary.

3. The first hurdle to answered prayer is learning about prayer, but not practicing it.

4. false; know

5. knowledge; spiritually

6. The best approach to prayer is to pray.

7. mental assent rather than action

8. Mental assent means intellectually accepting the Word as true—admiring it and agreeing with it—but not allowing it to have an impact on us, so that it doesn't do us any good. In essence, mental assent *agrees* with God but does not *believe* God.

9. doer; hearer

10. A variation of mental assent is sense knowledge. This is the attitude that says, "If I cannot see it, then it is not real. I'll believe it when I see it." Sense knowledge is a hurdle to overcome because it is not compatible with faith. The Bible tells us, *"We walk by faith, not by sight"* (2 Cor. 5:7 KJV). Faith is the substance and evidence of things that your sense knowledge cannot see. (See Hebrews 11:1.)

11. In many cultures, we are trained and conditioned to live by our five senses alone. If we cannot analyze something and empirically conclude that it actually works, then we do not believe it is real. God says that what He has promised is already a reality. Yet it won't become a *manifested* reality in our lives until we believe it is real *before* we see it—through fully trusting Him and His Word.

12. deceiving

13. The third hurdle is hearing the Word, but not absorbing it.

14. We undermine our spiritual health because we must internalize the Word if it is going to make an impact on our lives. When we don't absorb the Word, it often goes in one ear and out the other. Satan steals it away so that it can't have an impact on our relationship with God. (See Matthew 13:19.)

15. We will be blessed in what we do.

16. We absorb the Word by meditating on it, by staying focused after we've heard or read the Word, and letting it truly "sink into" our spirits.

17. Biblical meditation focuses on God's Word. It is not a mindless process of chanting but rather of *using* your mind—turning the Word over and over in your mind in order to understand all its truths and implications—and then embracing those truths by applying them to your whole life. Meditation may also be compared to the process of rumination,

such as when a cow chews its cud. First, you receive the Word by reading or hearing it. Then you "digest" it so that it can permeate your entire being and give you spiritual life and strength.

18. If Satan can steal the Word from us, he can steal what God has given us to fulfill His purposes in our lives. Satan never wants us to get to the meditation stage because that is when the Word of God can become the means for answered prayer.

19. The devil can't stop it because God now has something He can use in our lives to accomplish His will.

20. The fourth hurdle is hoping rather than having faith.

21. First, when we apply the biblical definition of hope (future fulfillment) to present-day faith situations. Second, when our hope is not the biblical kind but is really just wishful thinking.

22. Faith and hope are related but are distinct concepts. The Greek word for *"faith"* is *pistis,* meaning "belief" or "confidence." It can also mean "conviction" or "assurance." The word for *"hope"* is *elpis,* meaning "expectation" or "confidence." Biblical hope is *based* on faith because it is the confident anticipation of the ultimate fulfillment of that faith.

23. There are blessings God wants to give us in this life, in the present day. If we think these blessings are all in the future, we will not exercise our faith to see their fulfillment in our lives *now.* We will receive the future blessings for which we have faith and hope, but we will miss out on the blessings God wants to give us today.

24. (d) all of the above

25. We won't receive from the Lord what we desire.

26. praying for faith

27. When we pray for faith, we are praying to believe. Either we believe or we don't believe. Such a prayer is really based on unbelief, and therefore it will not be answered.

28. Faith grows as the Word is taken into our lives and acted upon. Romans 10:17 says, *"Faith comes from hearing the message, and the message is heard through the word of Christ."* Faith comes and increases as we hear and believe the Word and put it into practice.

29. True

30. God

31. Since *"faith comes from hearing...the word of Christ"* (Rom. 10:17), if we want to increase our faith, we must increase our intake of the Word of God. What we know of the Word becomes the limit of our faith because we can believe only what we know. We need to understand how God operates in every area of life because we need to have faith in all those areas.

32. The sixth hurdle is cares of the world/laziness. It involves neglecting prayer altogether, either through sheer laziness or because of life's busyness and distractions.

33. Whatever that person does know about prayer will not bear any fruit in his life.

Chapter Nine
Hindrances to Answered Prayer

1. Answers will vary.

2. The first major hindrance to answered prayer is sin.

3. We are separated from God, and He will not hear our prayers.

4. We receive what we ask of God when we keep God's commandments and do what is pleasing in His sight.

5. We should ask God to forgive us through Christ, and we should humble ourselves, pray, seek God's face, and turn from our sinful ways. When we do this, God will hear from heaven, forgive our sin, and bring healing. (See 1 John 2:1; 2 Chronicles 7:14.)

6. The second major hindrance is fear.

7. Fear often keeps us from believing we can approach God in prayer because we think He might remember a sin or failure on our part and/or we think He has something against us. In this way, fear hinders us from having freedom and confidence when we pray. Also, fear will block faith, and, thus, our prayers will be ineffective.

8. devil; other people; God

9. When we realize that God loved us and desired a relationship with us even when we didn't know Him and were living in sin, we will understand that we can freely come to Him and ask for forgiveness. If we confess our sin before God,

appropriating the cleansing blood of Jesus to purify us from all unrighteousness (see 1 John 1:9), then He will forgive us, and we can approach Him as if we had never sinned. God continues to forgive us through Christ even after we become Christians. Believers are in an even better position with God than nonbelievers in terms of not needing to fear. Romans 5:9 says, *"Since we have now been justified by his blood, how much more shall we be saved from God's wrath through him!"* God wants us to live with the assurance of forgiveness and move forward in His purposes with confidence.

10. guilt

11. Romans 8:1–2 tells us, *"Therefore, there is now no condemnation for those who are in Christ Jesus, because through Christ Jesus the law of the Spirit of life set me free from the law of sin and death."*

12. distrust

13. The devil uses our guilt to undermine our faith. Therefore, when we pray, our faith is weak, and our prayers aren't answered.

14. (b) blots out our transgressions and doesn't remember our sins.

15. The fourth major hindrance is feelings of inferiority. People are somehow ashamed of themselves and do not consider themselves worthy to receive what they are asking God for. When you have a low opinion of yourself, it is because you do not know God's true opinion of you, which he reveals in His Word.

16. Because of God's love for us, it was His pleasure and will to adopt us as His children; He lavishes His grace on us; He made known to us the mystery of His will—salvation through Christ; we were chosen in Christ.

17. enemy; incalculable

18. We should treat ourselves with respect and approach God as His chosen children. When we have the right estimation of ourselves as redeemed children of God, we don't come to prayer as someone who is begging. Instead, we confidently present our case. Prayer is not trying to get God to do something for us by making Him feel sorry for us. It is coming to Him knowing that we not only deserve what we ask because

of the righteousness of Christ, but we also have a right to it because it is based on His Word.

19. The fifth major hindrance is doubt.

20. The person who doubts is double-minded and unstable in everything he does.

21. We show we believe when we make specific preparations or arrangements for the answers to our prayers.

22. Wrong motives

23. Promoting our own egos and seeking selfish purposes or pleasures.

24. We should be asking God to fulfill His Word so that His kingdom can come on the earth.

25. False.

26. God meets our needs when our main focus is honoring God and promoting His purposes. When we have our priorities right, we can trust Him to meet our daily needs, as Jesus said in Matthew 6:33: *"Seek first his kingdom and his righteousness, and all these things will be given to you as well."*

27. The seventh major hindrance is bitterness.

28. Bitterness is holding something against someone and not releasing that person through forgiveness.

29. Bitterness hurts us more than the people against whom we are bitter. When we hold onto bitterness, it goes to the very source of our lives and dries it up. Not only will we be affected spiritually, but we will also begin to wither mentally, socially, and physically. It is like a cancer; it is an especially hideous, dangerous sin. *"See to it that no one misses the grace of God and that no bitter root grows up to cause trouble and defile many"* (Heb. 12:15).

30. The Bible says, *"If I regard iniquity in my heart, the Lord will not hear me"* (Ps. 66:18 KJV). Bitterness is iniquity, and iniquity is a vicious kind of sin, referring to perversity or moral evil, that God specifically says He hates. In Hebrews 1:9, we read, *"Thou hast loved righteousness, and hated iniquity"* (KJV). God says that if we willfully hold bitterness and similar sins in our hearts, it doesn't matter how long we pray; He won't hear us.

31. To guard against bitterness and keep our prayers from being hindered, we need to maintain transparent, pure hearts before God and man.

32. unforgiveness

33. Unforgiveness hinders our prayers by blocking our relationships with God and other people. First, God says that if we do not forgive others, our own sins will not be forgiven (Mark 11:25). Second, unforgiveness does not reflect the character of Christ, and it demonstrates ingratitude for the vast forgiveness God has extended to us. Jesus made this point very clear in the parable of the unforgiving servant in Matthew 18:23–35. Having an unimpeded relationship with God is linked to our extending forgiveness and love toward others.

34. The ninth major hindrance is broken family relationships.

35. As believers, we are to demonstrate the nature of God to one another. If we do not demonstrate the love, compassion, forgiveness, and grace of God to others, we are misrepresenting Him. We cannot ask Him to fulfill His purposes by answering our prayers when we are violating those very purposes by the way we treat others.

36. God wants us to mend the broken or hurting relationships in our homes so that our prayers won't be hindered. If we try to worship and praise God while ignoring the fact that our relationships are strained or estranged, our prayers will be ineffective. When God shows us that relationships need to be mended, we should yield to the Holy Spirit's prompting and make things right as soon as we can.

37. The tenth major hindrance is idols.

38. An idol of the heart is anything we give higher priority than God.

39. God deserves our primary love, respect, and devotion. Deuteronomy 6:5 says, *"Love the LORD your God with all your heart and with all your soul and with all your strength."*

40. stinginess

41. Proverbs 21:13 says, *"If a man shuts his ears to the cry of the poor, he too will cry out and not be answered."* This passage implies that we cannot ask God to provide for our needs when we're not concerned about the needs of those who are less fortunate than we are.

42. Proverbs 11:25: *"A generous man will prosper; he who refreshes others will himself be refreshed."* Proverbs 22:9: *"A*

generous man will himself be blessed, for he shares his food with the poor." Malachi 3:10: *"'Bring the whole tithe into the storehouse, that there may be food in my house. Test me in this,' says the LORD Almighty, 'and see if I will not throw open the floodgates of heaven and pour out so much blessing that you will not have room enough for it.'"*

Chapter Ten
The Power of the Word

1. Answers will vary.
2. Interwoven throughout this book has been the principle that we are to pray to God on the basis of His Word—the revelation of who He is, what His will is, and what He has promised.
3. purposed; predestined; establishment
4. motivation; content
5. Prayers that are based merely on our opinions, desires, and feelings, rather than on God's Word, are powerless to affect change.
6. properly; responsibly
7. God Himself is speaking in the Word, because the Word is who He is.
8. presence
9. foundation
10. The Word reveals God's nature—and it is His nature that reflects His will.
11. A cardinal principle of answered prayer is belief in the trustworthiness of the One to whom you're praying.
12. trust; action
13. The Word is alive. There is power in the Word because it is not just knowledge and facts to us; it is life itself.
14. God created the world through His Word; God's words to Abraham caused him to believe the covenant promise; God's words to Moses started him on the road to fulfilling his purpose and made him a successful leader; the word of the Lord came to Ezekiel many times and made him a powerful prophet; God redeemed the world through Jesus, the Word made flesh; the words of Jesus brought about salvation and

sanctification in His followers; Jesus' disciples continued His ministry on earth through the Word.

15. If we want the Word to work powerfully in our lives, we have to make sure it is inside us.

16. (1) Abiding in Jesus, and (2) Jesus' words abiding in us.

17. Abiding in Jesus means to constantly flow in spiritual communion with Him by fellowshipping with Him, worshipping Him, praying, and fasting.

18. The Word is truly abiding in us when it directs our thoughts and actions. For this to happen, we have to have the Word in us already. We have to be reading and meditating on the Word regularly.

19. If God's words are in us, then what we desire and ask for will reflect those words. If we are filled with the Word of God, then we won't ask for just anything we feel like. We will ask on the basis of His Word, which is what He watches over to fulfill. (See Jeremiah 1:12.)

20. The Word builds faith in us, which pleases God and causes Him to respond to our requests.

21. power

22. (d) all of the above

23. see

24. promise

25. open doors

26. When we pray God's Word, God hears Himself. And God will hear us when He hears the words He Himself has spoken.

27. We can know that we have what we asked God for.

28. Jesus said He didn't speak His own words, but the words the Father gave Him to say. (See John 12:49–50; John 14:10, 24.)

29. The Word says much about prayer. It builds faith in believers—and therefore gives power—because it is the greatest Book ever written about how God answers the faith-filled prayers of His people.

30. (c) were people just like us.

31. The people of the Old Testament received answers to their prayers as they put their faith in God, trusting in His character and Word, and God will do the same for us.

32. Christ's atonement, the prayers of Christ on our behalf, and the intercession of the Spirit for us.
33. The example of believers in the Bible can encourage us to have faith that God can and will intervene on our behalf.
34. The Word prepares the pray-er for prayer. It gives power in prayer by enabling us to be ready for it and maintain communion with God.
35. When we wholeheartedly embrace the Word, it keeps our lives in line with God's will so that nothing will hinder us from walking in His ways and receiving answers to our prayers.
36. We need to offer our lives to God every day as living sacrifices, holy and pleasing to Him.
37. As our minds are transformed by reading and meditating on the Word, and by living according to it instead of according to the pattern of this world, we will know the will of God, which will enable us to pray confidently and effectively.

Chapter Eleven
The Power of Jesus' Name

1. Answers will vary.
2. False. It's not the word *Jesus* but what the name represents that makes the difference. We're not effective in prayer just by using the name of Jesus, but in understanding the significance of who He really is and appropriating His power through faith in His name.
3. First, we must be in proper relationship with Christ. Second, we must understand how to use Jesus' name.
4. We have a covenantal authority based on our covenant relationship with God through the redemption of Christ.
5. John 16:23–27
6. God; men; Satan
7. In the Scriptures, the name of someone (or something) usually symbolized the essence of his nature. It represented the person's collective attributes and characteristics—his nature, power, and glory.
8. it *is* who He is
9. God's overarching name, I Am, encompasses all His nature and attributes. God is saying, in effect, "I *am* My name. My

name is whatever I am at the time I am it." This is because God is everything we need. His name differs depending on what our need is at a particular time. Whatever we need, we can call on God in that capacity.

10. God is affirming that He is a personal God who meets individual human needs. He is the God of real people.

11. Son of God; Son of Man

12. I Am; Jesus

13. *"'I tell you the truth,' Jesus answered, 'before Abraham was born, I am!'"* (John 8:58).

14. We must pray based on the divine name that meets our particular need at the time.

15. problem; attribute

16. Dr. Munroe said that we lose many things in life because we declare them dead prematurely. At times we will confront situations that look final, but God will resurrect them because Jesus is the Resurrection.

17. Legally, when you give power of attorney to someone, it means that you appoint that person to represent you. You give the person the legal right and authority to speak for you and to do business in your name. Praying in the name of Jesus is giving Him power of attorney to intercede on our behalf when we make requests of the Father.

18. The Father works through Christ.

19. Jesus is actively working on our behalf from His position at the right hand of the Father. (See Romans 8:34.)

20. *"Therefore he is able to save completely those who come to God through him, because he always lives to intercede for them"* (Heb. 7:25).

21. Jesus will answer requests prayed in His name in faith *"so that the Son may bring glory to the Father."*

22. The Holy Spirit assists in exercising power of attorney by enabling us to pray as we present our cases to God. He helps us get our situations clearly sorted out so we can present them to the Father in Jesus' name. This is especially true when we do not know what we should be praying for. (See Romans 8:26–27.)

23. (c) not ask for what we were going to ask. The correct answer is "c" because we cannot present something to the

Father if the timing is not right, or if it is out of God's will for our lives altogether. The Holy Spirit will not prompt us to pray for something in Jesus' name if we are not praying according to God's purposes.

24. Jesus said, *"The Father loves the Son"* (John 3:35; 5:20). Because the Father loves the Son, and they are unified in heart and purpose, He will do what the Son asks.

25. heaven

26. True

27. *"For there is one God and one mediator between God and men, the man Christ Jesus"* (1 Tim. 2:5).

28. Jesus' name is power in heaven. Every tongue will eventually confess that He is Lord—Lord of everything. Jesus is Lord over every problem, need, and purpose in our lives, and we can address all these issues in the power of His name. The authority of Jesus' name is also the basis on which we are to fulfill the Great Commission with courage and boldness. (See Matthew 28:18–19.)

Chapter Twelve
Understanding Fasting

1. Answers will vary.

2. Answers will vary.

3. True

4. equal parts; single

5. Jesus used the words **"When** *you pray..."* and **"When** *you fast..."* (Matthew 6:5–6, 16–17, emphasis added). He didn't say, "If you pray..." and "If you fast...." He expected fasting to be practiced by God's people.

6. False. There are times when the Holy Spirit will move upon a person or group of people and supernaturally give them a desire to fast. Yet the majority of the time, fasting is an act of our faith and our wills. It is a decision we make based on our obedience to and love for Christ.

7. A fast is a conscious, intentional decision to abstain for a time from the pleasure of eating in order to gain vital spiritual benefits.

8. The first purpose of fasting is for seeking God.

9. whole heart
10. The second purpose of fasting is for putting God first.
11. By focusing all our attention on Him alone—not on His gifts or blessings, but on God Himself. This shows God how much we love and appreciate Him; we are seeking Him above everyone and everything else in life.
12. Fasting is a point of intimacy with God because God will reveal Himself only to people who truly want to know Him. He says, *"You will seek me and find me when you seek me with all your heart"* (Jer. 29:13).
13. creating an environment for prayer
14. In the Bible, we see examples of the Israelites fasting in conjunction with wholehearted prayer to God in times of mourning and repentance in which they sought and received God's mercy. Fasting was also used as a point of deliverance when the Israelites sought God's wisdom and help in defeating their enemies, and God came to their aid.
15. The fourth purpose of fasting is for interceding for others.
16. The main purpose of fasting is to benefit others (rather than ourselves).
17. Fasting goes beyond just praying because sometimes our prayers can be very selfish. We often pray only for our own wants and needs. Fasting takes prayer into a completely different realm by focusing on the needs of others.
18. empty; fill
19. (d) all of the above
20. True
21. The first result we receive is hearing from God. Fasting allows us to receive guidance, wisdom, instruction, and knowledge from God.
22. The second result we receive is power from God. Fasting enables us to receive the fullness of God's power for ministry.
23. There are some things for which we need to be especially prepared to deal with spiritually. At such times, we need a spirit of special consecration to God and an abstinence from physical pleasures such as eating, which can interfere with the flow of God's power in our lives. Fasting helps to facilitate these things.

24. Although we receive the Holy Spirit when we are born again, our spirits need to be frequently renewed by God's Spirit, as Jesus' was through fasting and prayer. A fast ignites the Spirit's power within us so that our love, devotion, and service for God have new zeal and power.

25. After fasting, we are equipped to deal with such situations and people through the power of the Spirit.

26. The third result we receive is breakthroughs in difficult situations.

27. Answers may vary, but should include the following ideas: The Israelites needed to show their complete dependence upon God by sincerely repenting of their sins and consecrating themselves anew to Him. As they drew near to Him, He would draw near to them and provide the deliverance and blessings they needed.

28. In Joel 2:12–13, God tells us that if we repent, fast, and return to Him, He is *"gracious and compassionate, slow to anger and abounding in love, and he relents from sending calamity."* In the same chapter, He talks about the spiritual and material blessings that He gives when His people turn to Him with their whole hearts. (See verses 18–32.)

29. Answers may vary, but should include the following ideas: *Right ways to fast:* Being consecrated and committed to God, fasting while having the right priorities, lifting people's burdens, having the heart of a giver, showing love to others, and having a burden for souls. *Wrong ways to fast:* Fasting while treating others with injustice, quarreling and striving, pursuing our own pleasures rather than God's will.

30. The results of a true fast are that people are delivered and restored to God, and the one who fasts receives God's blessings (such as healing and protection).

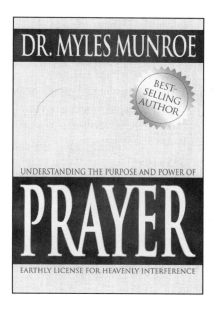

DR. MYLES MUNROE

BEST-SELLING AUTHOR

UNDERSTANDING THE PURPOSE AND POWER OF

PRAYER

EARTHLY LICENSE FOR HEAVENLY INTERFERENCE

Understanding the Purpose and Power of Prayer
Dr. Myles Munroe

All that God is—and all that God has—may be received
through prayer. Everything you need to fulfill your purpose on
earth is available to you through prayer. The biblically based,
time-tested principles presented here by Dr. Myles Munroe
will ignite and transform the way you pray. Be prepared to
enter into a new dimension of faith, a deeper revelation of
God's love, and a renewed understanding that
you can pray—and receive results.

ISBN: 0-88368-442-X • Trade • 240 pages

ய
WHITAKER
HOUSE

The Principles and Power of Vision
Dr. Myles Munroe

Whether you are a businessperson, a homemaker, a student, or a head of state, best-selling author Dr. Myles Munroe explains how you can make your dreams and hopes a living reality. Your success is not dependent on the state of the economy or what the job market is like. You do not need to be hindered by the limited perceptions of others or by a lack of resources. Discover time-tested principles that will enable you to fulfill your vision no matter who you are or where you come from. You were not meant for a mundane or mediocre life. Revive your passion for living, pursue your dream, discover your vision—and find your true life.

ISBN: 0-88368-951-0 • Hardcover • 240 pages

WU
WHITAKER
HOUSE

proclaiming the power of the Gospel through the written word
visit our website at www.whitakerhouse.com